More advance praise for *The Cultural Intelligence Difference*

"Being 'international' is not defined by the stamp in your passport; it is what happens after you 'get there' that defines your ability to understand and adapt to different cultures and different approaches to common concerns. Living and breathing international 24/7, I would describe Livermore's concept as not just applicable in today's world, but brilliant, and not a minute too soon. *The Cultural Intelligence Difference* is a must-read for adults and should be a mandatory read as a part of a secondary or undergraduate education."

—**Mary Jean Eisenhower,** President and CEO, People to People International, and granddaughter of President Eisenhower

"As companies globalize more and more, working across cultures is becoming a critical competency for executives everywhere. This is one of the best books to attack the question of how to measure and improve this key competency."

—**David Rock,** cofounder, NeuroLeadership Institute, and author, *Your Brain at Work*

"The case for Cultural Intelligence in all interactions with people who are different is paramount today and in the future. David has made a critical competence for effectiveness in global engagements more easily understood."

—**Geri P. Thomas,** Senior Vice President, Global Diversity and Inclusion Executive, Bank of America

"Written so the common man can understand and digest, this brilliantly crafted book on Cultural Intelligence explains how to engage with the 'other' rather than just observing from afar. Using brilliant everyday examples, Dr. Livermore explains how you can take practical steps to become a first-class global citizen!"

—**Wilbur Sargunaraj,** Performing Artist, Humanitarian, and Global Ambassador for CQ

THE CULTURAL INTELLIGENCE DIFFERENCE

THE CULTURAL
INTELLIGENCE DIFFERENCE

*Master the One Skill You Can't Do Without
in Today's Global Economy*

DAVID LIVERMORE, Ph.D.

AMACOM
American Management Association
New York • Atlanta • Brussels • Chicago • Mexico City • San Francisco
Shanghai • Tokyo • Toronto • Washington, D.C.

Bulk discounts available. For details visit:
www.amacombooks.org/go/specialsales
Or contact special sales:
Phone: 800-250-5308
E-mail: specialsls@amanet.org
View all the AMACOM titles at: www.amacombooks.org

This publication is designed to provide accurate and authoritative information in regard to the subject matter covered. It is sold with the understanding that the publisher is not engaged in rendering legal, accounting, or other professional service. If legal advice or other expert assistance is required, the services of a competent professional person should be sought.

Library of Congress Cataloging-in-Publication Data
Livermore, David A., 1967–
   The cultural intelligence difference: master the one skill you can't do without in today's global economy / David Livermore.
        p. cm.
   Includes index.
   ISBN-13: 978-0-8144-1706-5 (hbk.)
   ISBN-10: 0-8144-1706-X (hbk.)
   1. Diversity in the workplace. 2. Cultural intelligence. 3. Intercultural communication. 4. Management—Cross-cultural studies. 5. Organizational behavior—Cross-cultural studies. I. Title.
   HF5549.5.M5L58 2011
   650.1'3—dc22   2010043843

ABOUT AMA
American Management Association (www.amanet.org) is a world leader in talent development, advancing the skills of individuals to drive business success. Our mission is to support the goals of individuals and organizations through a complete range of products and services, including classroom and virtual seminars, webcasts, webinars, podcasts, conferences, corporate and government solutions, business books, and research. AMA's approach to improving performance combines experiential learning—learning through doing—with opportunities for ongoing professional growth at every step of one's career journey.

Printing number
10 9 8 7 6 5 4 3 2 1

To Linda, Emily, and Grace, my cherished ones.

CONTENTS

This book is devoted to helping you make the most of today's multicultural, globalized world. You'll learn how to improve your cultural intelligence, or CQ—an evidence-based way to be effective in any cross-cultural situation.

PART I

AN INTRODUCTION TO CQ

See how cultural intelligence is uniquely suited for not only surviving the crazy demands of our globalized world but also thriving in them.

PART II

STRATEGIES TO IMPROVE YOUR CQ

PART III

CONCLUDING THOUGHTS

See how CQ is helping individuals and organizations successfully accomplish their objectives and simultaneously make the world a better place.

Turn the ideas of these pages into reality. It isn't easy, but the results are well worth the hard work. Use CQ to discover the possibilities awaiting you in today's borderless world.

PREFACE

The number one predictor of your success in today's borderless world is not your IQ, not your resume, and not even your expertise. It's your CQ, a powerful capability that is proven to enhance your effectiveness working in culturally diverse situations. And CQ is something anyone can develop and learn. Research conducted in more than thirty countries over the last decade has shown that people with high CQ are better able to adjust and adapt to the unpredictable, complex situations of life and work in today's globalized world.[1]

CQ or cultural intelligence is the capability to function effectively in a variety of cultural contexts—including national, ethnic, organizational, and generational. It's a whole new way of approaching the age-old topics of cultural sensitivity, racism, and cross-border effectiveness. And it will open up a whole new world of possibilities for you. The purpose of this book is to improve your cultural intelligence. Welcome to *The CQ Difference!*

I never actually left the continent until I was in college, but I've been intrigued by cultural differences for as long as I can remember. My parents moved from Canada to the United States shortly before I was born. Multiple times a year we made treks across the Canadian border to visit my grandparents and cousins. I was intrigued by the different money, the varied ways of saying things, and the different foods that existed on just the other side of Niagara Falls. Once I started kindergarten, my American classmates laughed when I said "mum" or "eh." And my Canadian cousins accused me of becoming an arrogant, flag-waving American. With youthful patriotism I rebutted, "Well at least we don't still bow to the queen!"

Many years later, I've had the privilege of traveling all over the world. The excitement of getting on a plane has long dissipated, but landing in a new place hasn't. Few things get my adrenaline flowing like scouting out a new place, roaming the streets, eating the local food, and soaking in everything I can. Like anyone who has traveled internationally, I've made more than my fair share of cultural gaffes and blunders. But those are some of the best ways I've gotten better at working and relating cross-culturally.[2]

Cultural intelligence, however, runs so much deeper than discovering new foods, languages, and currencies. It strikes right at the core of our beliefs and convictions. My journey from my Canadian-American home to a life of worldwide travel has been fun and fulfilling. The journey of rethinking my faith, ideals, and opinions has been much more disorienting and painful, albeit deeply rewarding in its own way.

Like many people, I grew up with an insulated view of the world. Our family's social network revolved around people like us. We associated with people who looked like us, shared our religious beliefs, affirmed our political perspectives, and defined success and failure like we did. We were convinced our way was the one right way to view the world.

But the more I encountered people who saw the world differently from us, the more suspect I became of our way being the only right way to interpret reality. I began to wonder, *Can't we still live out our values and convictions without automatically presuming our way is what's right and best for everyone?*

I'm forty-three now. The simplistic categories of "us" versus "them" don't work for me anymore. To be sure, this is an ongoing journey for me. I don't know how to think about the world without some set of universal morals, whether it's the preservation of life, caring for our young, or apprehending evil oppressors. But the more I encounter the diversity of the world, the more challenged I become with how I arrive at my own points of view. I'm not interested in some vanilla tolerance that just nods in agreement with everything I hear. Instead, let's have a rigorous debate with a true openness to hearing one another's ideas and perspectives. CQ is more than just a technique for cross-cultural work. It transforms the way I teach, parent, watch the news, discuss issues, work with colleagues, and grow in my friendships.

I've tried to write a book that provides simple strategies for improving your CQ. The strategies themselves are things any of us can apply and use. But I'd be remiss if I didn't acknowledge that underlying these strategies is a willingness to undergo a transformation in how we see ourselves, the people we encounter, and the world at large. This kind of change takes many years and can be disorientating, frustrating, and painful. However, the benefits far outweigh the cost.

* * *

We begin in Chapter 1 with a brief introduction of how cultural intelligence is proven to help you succeed in the midst of the cultural challenges and demands of our rapidly globalizing world. Chapter 2 will give you an overview of the cultural intelligence research and its origins.

With the purchase of this book, you also have access to the CQ Self-Assessment. To date, this is the only academically tested CQ assessment in the world. You can take the assessment at any time, but I recommend you do so after reading Chapters 1 and 2.

Chapters 3 to 6 provide dozens of proven strategies for improving your CQ. Previous books about cultural intelligence, including my own, have mostly focused on *what* CQ is. This one is devoted to *how you can improve your CQ*. After completing the online *CQ Self-Assessment*, you can better determine where to begin work on increasing your CQ based on your highest and lowest scores. The strategies in this section are all things I've used and personally benefited from. But that's not why you should pay attention to them. They are important strategies because they have emerged from rigorous research conducted by academics around the world.

Chapter 7 describes the power of CQ by synthesizing the key strengths of the CQ approach and sharing some inspirational stories of individuals and organizations who are harnessing the power of CQ in their multicultural pursuits. Growing numbers of organizations and leaders are using these findings to increase their effectiveness in reaching their bottom-line objectives and as a way to make the world a better place. That's what compels me to give so much of my energy to the cultural intelligence work. I truly believe that if you use the strategies in this book, you'll not only survive the challenges of our twenty-first-century world, you'll thrive in the midst of them and tap into the possibilities waiting to be discovered in our changing world. That's the CQ difference!

Welcome to the emerging domain of cultural intelligence. It's a whole new way of seeing the world.

David Livermore
Grand Rapids, Michigan

PART I

AN INTRODUCTION TO CQ

Cultural intelligence might sound like a really academic, intellectual topic. It is rooted in years of scholarly research conducted by academics in places around the world. But it's easy to grasp, and the findings offer benefits to all of us.

In the next two chapters, you'll gain insight into how cultural intelligence connects with you and your interests. And you'll discover research findings that show how increasing your CQ will improve your effectiveness at whatever you set out to do in today's borderless world.

CHAPTER 1

CQ FOR YOU

Your success in today's globalized world requires an ability to adapt to a variety of cultural situations. Conventional wisdom has been telling us this for decades. But only in recent years have academics discovered a proven way to quantify and develop this ability. It's called *cultural intelligence*, or *CQ*, and it's defined as the capability to function effectively in a variety of cultural contexts. All kinds of people are discovering the possibilities that CQ opens up for them. But improving your cultural intelligence does require some commitment and intentionality on your part. Rest easy. The rewards are well worth the effort.

The world is shrinking. Today, we're connected to people from around the globe more than ever before. Fifty years ago, you could have lived most of your life surrounded by people who looked like you, believed like you, and saw the world pretty much the same way you do. A few individuals still manage to pull that off. But most of us encounter and work with people who look, believe, and think in radically different ways from us. We've learned that we don't need to become like whomever we're with. But our effectiveness and success is largely dependent on our ability to adapt to various cultural contexts. When we learn to effectively and respectfully interact with people from diverse cultures, we strike a gold mine of opportunity for personal and professional fulfillment.

The shifting realities of our rapidly globalized world are well documented in best-selling books like *The World Is Flat* by Thomas Friedman and *One World* by Peter Singer. Most of us are well aware that globalization and worldwide connectivity are lunging forward with racing speed. Here are a few examples:

- 1 billion tourist visas are issued annually, and the number keeps rising.[1]

- General Electric calculates that 60 percent of its growth over the coming decade will come from the developing world, compared with 20 percent over the past decade.[2]

- 49 percent of U.S. kids five and younger are children of color.[3]

- China will soon be the number-one English-speaking country in the world.

- 67 percent of international air travel revenue is generated by Asian and Middle Eastern airlines, and the percentage is growing annually.[4]

- More than 1 million university students study abroad annually.

- 4.5 million North Americans participate in religious international mission trips each year.[5]

I doubt you'd pick up a book on cultural intelligence if you weren't already convinced of our global and multicultural connectivity. But this is a book about you and your life in our borderless world. To what degree do you possess the capabilities needed to succeed in this cultural mosaic? Why do some of us succeed while others fail at cross-cultural effectiveness?

Intercultural success has little to do with your IQ or EQ (emotional intelligence). It's primarily dependent on your CQ. Everyone has a cultural intelligence quotient (CQ), and we can all improve our CQ. This book, along with the corresponding online *CQ Self-Assessment*, will enable you to understand your CQ and give you the latest tested strategies for improving it.

WHAT IS CULTURAL INTELLIGENCE?

Again, cultural intelligence is the *capability to function effectively across a variety of cultural contexts*, such as ethnic, generational, and organizational cultures. CQ has some similarities with various approaches to cultural competence, but it differs in its specific ties to intelligence research. As a result, the emphasis is not only on understanding different cultures, but also on problem solving and effective adaptations for various cultural settings. By using the "intelligence" approach, the CQ model also acknowledges that your multicultural interactions are as much *personal, individualized experiences* as they are simply knowing about differences between Germans and Koreans. Even if you and I have the same cultural background, we'll experience new cross-cultural situations differently according to who we are as individuals.

CQ is an overall capability you can take with you anywhere. You can benefit from its insights even if you're experiencing a culture for the first time, unlike approaches that place primary emphasis on learning all the dos and don'ts of specific cultures. You can use CQ to become better relating to neighbors, classmates, and colleagues who come from another part of the world, or you can use it to increase the chances your meme goes viral throughout the world. You'll evaluate your CQ a little later when you complete the online *CQ Self-Assessment* included with this book. High CQ doesn't come automatically, but anyone can develop it.

Throughout the last ten years, most of the discussion about cultural intelligence has been buried in academic journals. Some of these studies are really fascinating; unfortunately, most of us never see them. For example, one study found that an individual with multiple international working experiences, even if those experiences were relatively brief, is likely to have higher CQ than an individual who has lived overseas for several years in one or two locations.[6] And neurological studies find that the brain gets wired differently depending upon one's intercultural experiences, which in turn impacts the way the individual approaches problem solving and day-to-day work.[7] These kinds of findings have significant implications for how individuals and organizations maximize global opportunities. We'll look at many more of these findings in the chapters that follow.

During the last couple of years, CQ has started to go mainstream. Growing numbers of leaders in business, government, and nonprofit organizations are realizing the benefits that come from this intelligence-based approach to adapting and working cross-culturally. And many corporations, government agencies, and universities are tapping into the CQ difference to achieve results. A few specific examples are included in Chapter 7.

Your cultural intelligence is made up of four different capabilities, each of which is assessed in the online *CQ Self-Assessment*.

1. **CQ Drive (motivation)** is your *interest and confidence in functioning effectively in culturally diverse settings*. This often gets overlooked. Without the ample drive to take

on the challenges that inevitably accompany multicultural situations, there's little evidence you'll be successful.

2. **CQ Knowledge (cognition)** is your *knowledge about how cultures are similar and different.* The emphasis is not on being an expert about every culture you encounter. That's overwhelming and impossible. Instead, to what extent do you understand some core cultural differences and their impact on you and others?

3. **CQ Strategy (meta-cognition)** is how you *make sense of culturally diverse experiences.* It occurs when you make judgments about your own thought processes and those of others. Can you plan effectively in light of cultural differences?

4. **CQ Action (behavior)** is your *capability to adapt your behavior appropriately for different cultures.* It involves having a flexible repertoire of responses to suit various situations while still remaining true to yourself.

Together, these four capabilities make up your overall cultural intelligence quotient. The online *CQ Self-Assessment* will reveal which of these capabilities is strongest and weakest for you. But what's your best guess? As you read the four descriptions, which one seems like it's the strongest for you? What about the weakest? After you complete the *CQ Self-Assessment*, you'll be able to tap into pinpointed strategies that are proven to enhance your CQ. Before you do so, here's a bit more about the CQ model.

WHAT DOES HIGH CULTURAL INTELLIGENCE LOOK LIKE?

Despite its academic origins, cultural intelligence is pretty easy to grasp. Everyone can improve their CQ. I want to help you become more successful as you pursue the things most important to you in our borderless world. Having a high CQ doesn't mean exhibiting flawless behavior in cross-cultural settings. Instead, it is personified by people with a strong sense of their own cultural identity. They know who they are and what they believe, but they're equally interested to discover that in others. And individuals with high CQ have an integrated view of the world that appreciates both the similarities and differences among people. Rather than being threatened by differences, they look for what they can learn from them.

Here's one way of thinking about the progression from low CQ (1.0) to high CQ (5.0):

1.0—You react to external stimuli (what you see and hear, etc., in a new cultural context) and you judge it based on what that means in your own cultural context.

> *Example:* You observe that some individuals are silent during a meeting and you presume they're using the "silent treatment" to demonstrate they're bored and upset.

2.0—You begin to recognize other cultural norms. You're motivated to learn more about how cultures differ.

> *Example:* You observe that some individuals are silent during a meeting and you wonder if remaining silent means the same thing in their culture as it means in yours.

3.0—You begin to accommodate other cultural norms into your thinking. You can explain how culture impacts the way people might respond differently to the same circumstances.

> *Example:* You observe that some individuals are silent during a meeting and you decide to explore whether their silence is a form of respect, as it is in many cultures.

4.0—You adapt and adjust your thinking and behavior to other cultural norms.

Example: You observe that some individuals are silent during a meeting and you intentionally ask for their input, believing they might consider it disrespectful to offer it unless invited to give it.

5.0—You automatically adjust your thinking and behavior when you get appropriate cues, sometimes subconsciously.

Example: You observe that some individuals are silent during a meeting and, almost without thinking about it, you offer them alternative ways to offer input; you're subconsciously aware that their cultural background typically uses silence as a form of respect.

Nobody behaves flawlessly in cross-cultural interactions. And frankly, the mistakes we make are often the best teachers for improving our CQ. But with experience and intentional effort, we can move toward the CQ 5.0 description where we begin to automatically accommodate a variety of behaviors and strategies into the ways we work with people from different cultural backgrounds. As you grow your CQ, you'll gradually be able to interpret the behavior of people from unfamiliar cultures as if you were an insider in their cultures.

Low CQ is often easier to spot because faux pas are more interesting to talk about. For example, the Dairy Association led a wildly successful marketing campaign throughout the United States built on the slogan, "Got Milk?" Unfortunately, when the campaign was exported to Mexico, the translation read, "Are you lactating?"[8]

People with low CQ will dismiss the seismic influence of culture on themselves and others. They may use overly simplistic approaches to working cross-culturally and make statements such as, "People are people. A smile and kind word work anywhere." Furthermore, many business leaders with lower levels of CQ use disjointed, slap-dash approaches to the myriad of cultural forces barraging them—whom to send overseas, how to create a more innovative culture, how to extend into more emerging markets, how to read trends in their own culture, HR policies, etc.

Low CQ is a primary reason many businesses continue to lose millions of dollars when expanding into culturally diverse markets. It explains why many charitable organizations get kicked out of developing nations because of their inability to work with local officials in addressing atrocities like HIV-AIDS or human trafficking. The globalization of every field is lunging forward at an unprecedented rate, yet 70 percent of international programs in business, government, and charity are largely ineffective and costly.[9] But it doesn't have to be that way.

Individuals with high CQ have a repertoire of strategies and behaviors to orient themselves when they encounter unfamiliar behaviors and perspectives. When something seemingly bizarre or random happens, they have a mental frame to discern whether it's explained by culture or it's something unique to a particular person or organization. With enhanced CQ, you have the ability to encounter new cultural situations, think deeply about what's happening (or not happening), and make appropriate adjustments to how you should understand, relate, and behave in these otherwise-disorienting situations. For example:

- Teachers with high CQ learn how to adapt their teaching, assessment, and feedback strategies when working with students from various cultural backgrounds.

- Human resource managers with higher levels of CQ have a better sense of how to handle a Muslim employee's request to miss a sales conference during Ramadan.

- Hospitals led by culturally intelligent leaders are more effective at treating immigrant patients and have fewer lawsuits due to misdiagnosis of those patients.

- Students with higher CQ who volunteer or study abroad gain more long-term benefits from the experience.

- Liberals and conservatives with high CQ temper their broad, sweeping statements about one another, seek to understand the other party's position, and learn where the true differences lie rather than sensationalizing artificial polarities.

These kinds of adjustments involve a complex set of capabilities that stem from enhanced cultural intelligence. Anyone can grow his or her CQ. It doesn't happen automatically, but with a little effort, you can experience several benefits by increasing your CQ.

WHAT ARE THE BENEFITS OF INCREASING YOUR CQ?

Sometimes capabilities like emotional and cultural intelligence get written off as soft skills with limited, tangible benefit for life in the real world. Business leaders with low CQ might see discussions about culture as far removed from the P&L sheets that determine their survival. A naive military leader might believe cultural intelligence has little impact on a strategic combat mission. And study-abroad students with low CQ may view conversations with locals as irrelevant to their purposes for being overseas. These attitudes miss the hard-core, bottom-line differences that exist for individuals who prioritize enhancing their cultural intelligence.

A growing number of individuals, however, are discovering the competitive edge that comes from enhancing their CQ. Scientific research reveals that the most predictable results you can expect from increasing your cultural intelligence are the following:

- Superior cross-cultural adjustment

- Improved job performance

- Enhanced personal well-being

- Greater profitability

Let's look further at these benefits.

Cross-Cultural Adjustment

Most twenty-first-century interests, jobs, and causes require adjustment to various cultures. The demand for this is going to grow exponentially over the next decade. What's your passion?

- *Business?* Some of the most profitable opportunities lie in new offshore markets and stem from synergizing and motivating culturally diverse work teams.

- *Investment?* Intercultural sensibilities are a huge asset for making the most of our globalized economy.

- *Teaching?* Classrooms are increasingly filled with a diversity of students who need to be prepared for life in our globalized world.

- *Leadership?* There's hardly anything a leader touches that isn't shaped by culture, including vision casting, managing people, and developing a strategic plan.

- *Making the world a better place?* Whether your cause is HIV-AIDS prevention, animal rights, environmental sustainability, or mentoring kids in the inner city, charitable activities are rife with the need for cross-cultural adaptability.

Music, sports, travel, religion, research, technology, science, farming, raising a family, politics, filmmaking—I'm hard pressed to think of a pursuit in today's world that doesn't involve some need to interact with and adapt to people and situations of various cultural backgrounds. And the greater your cultural intelligence, the more likely you are to successfully adjust to the cultures you encounter in whatever you pursue.[10]

In fact, your cultural intelligence has more to do with your success in these kinds of multicultural endeavors than your age, gender, location, IQ, or EQ. Multicultural situations are filled with ambiguity. We're often unaware when a problem arises, and we miss what is really happening. Enhanced CQ provides the motivation, understanding, and strategy for dealing with that uncertainty. Sometimes, individuals presume they can't be successful in multicultural situations because they've grown up in a very monocultural context or because they're too "old."

That's not true! We can all improve our CQ, and an enhanced CQ is far more likely to contribute to successfully adjusting cross-culturally than your age or where you're from.[11] Men and women can be equally successful in multicultural situations. Your effectiveness is more a result of your CQ than your gender. And if you've never been at the top of your class, take heart: Your CQ is more likely to predict your intercultural work and relationships than your academic achievement or IQ. EQ is a strong predictor of your success when you're working with people who come from the same culture as you, but your CQ is a much better predictor of how you'll do working with people from different cultural backgrounds—the inevitable reality for all of us over the next decade.

One reason you'll more likely succeed with enhanced CQ is that cultural intelligence contributes to increased flexibility. If you've ever participated in any kind of cross-cultural training, you've been told again and again about the need to be flexible. But rarely are we offered specific training and skills in how to truly adapt. Instead, the mantra is just repeated, "Be flexible. Expect the unexpected. Be flexible, and then flex some more."

Okay—but how?

As individuals grow in cultural intelligence, there's a direct correlation with their ability to adapt to various situations and environments where the assumptions, values, and traditions differ from those with which they're most familiar. For example, research shows that people with higher levels of CQ work more effectively with multicultural teams than leaders with lower levels of CQ do and, therefore, they have more success in forming collaborative environments across a diversity of cultures. In the coming decades, this kind of capability will become nonnegotiable for anyone in management.[12]

One of the realities of living in such a rapidly globalizing world is that an ability to respectfully and effectively connect with individuals and situations from various cultural backgrounds is required of all of us. Enhanced CQ helps you be more effective at whatever you pursue.

> **Research Note:** The relationship between CQ and an individual's adjustment cross-culturally was much stronger than the relationship between an individual's age, experience, gender, location, or IQ with their cross-cultural success.[13]

Job Performance

With higher CQ you'll also have an edge in a crowded job market. Even if a position doesn't require any international travel, managers and HR departments are realizing the importance of having culturally savvy employees who can dynamically meet the challenges of serving a diverse customer base at home and abroad, as well as becoming effective participants of culturally diverse teams. In addition, employers are finding that personnel with high CQ are not only more effective cross-culturally but also are more adaptable and innovative as they go about tasks within their own cultural contexts. Growing numbers of companies are assessing the CQ of job candidates and existing workers. Dozens of academic studies have discovered the connections between higher CQ and better job performance. Some of the most important job-related results for individuals with higher CQ are in the following areas:

- *Decision Making.* One reason why CQ increases your job performance is that it results in better judgment and decision making. Individuals who lead with their gut and intuitively go with the flow are often caught off guard by situations that yield unpredictable results when working cross-culturally. Individuals with higher CQ are better at anticipating and managing risk and at making decisions that involve complex, multicultural dynamics. Cultural intelligence will help you make better decisions.[14]

- *Negotiation.* Being able to negotiate effectively across cultures is cited as one of the most important competencies needed in today's global workplace. Individuals with higher CQ are more successful at cross-cultural negotiations than individuals with lower CQ. When faced with the ambiguity of intercultural communication, with high CQ, you're more likely to persist and invest great effort in reaching a win–win despite the absence of cues that help you negotiate effectively in a more familiar environment. Heightened CQ will give you a better understanding of how to read the nonverbal cues during a negotiation and make you more aware of how to motivate an individual or company from a different culture.[15]

- *Networking.* Networking is another one of the most sought-after skills in today's work environment. Individuals who can successfully network and build relationships with individuals and organizations that span geographic, cultural, and ethnic boundaries are in high demand. CQ will enhance your ability to network effectively across varied contexts. Anthropologist Grant McCracken tells his fellow baby boomers, "It's the network, stupid!" He writes, "My generation treated the corporation as a source of security. [Gen Y] has another source of security. As long as they have their social network, the place they work matters much less."[16] Networks are the currency that matters in today's global environment. Military operations that require multinational peacekeeping efforts and companies that depend on creative mergers and acquisitions are best facilitated by individuals who can build multicultural networks. High CQ will help you do this.[17]

- *Global Leadership Effectiveness.* Finally, today's managers need to effectively hire, motivate, and develop personnel from a variety of cultures. Even if you don't aspire to a primary leadership role, your job performance may require that you effectively influence and develop teams of culturally diverse participants. With higher levels of CQ, you're more likely to develop trust and effectively lead multicultural groups and projects at home or dispersed around the world.[18]

> **Research Note:** Organizations want to hire individuals with high CQ because employees with high CQ are better decision makers, negotiators, networkers, and leaders for today's globalized world.[19]

Personal Well-Being

Enhancing your cultural intelligence is proven to enhance your personal satisfaction and overall well-being, particularly when engaging in culturally diverse situations. When you enhance your cultural intelligence, you're less likely to experience burnout from the constant demands faced by multicultural interactions. We all want to be effective at what we do. Fatigue and stress are inevitable challenges that accompany cross-cultural encounters, so anything that helps reduce the fatigue and stress is welcome.

Growth in CQ leads to reduced stress for individuals who interact with a large number of cross-cultural situations regularly. People such as immigration officers, refugee placement workers, short-term business travelers, and social workers working in urban contexts are under a great deal of stress, given the challenges associated with cross-cultural work. Professionals with higher levels of cultural intelligence are less likely to burn out from this kind of work than those with lower levels of cultural intelligence. For example, many short-term business travelers are expected to fly in and out of many different places from month to month. It's impossible to master the proper norms for every culture encountered, but with cultural intelligence, a decent measure of respect and effectiveness is possible. Many managers work all day long to bridge different cultures and find themselves mentally exhausted by being the interpreter between various generational, professional, and ethnic subcultures. Those with higher levels of cultural intelligence experience less burnout from a litany of multicultural encounters.[20]

Employees with higher levels of CQ also report a greater level of enjoyment from traveling and working internationally than those with lower levels of CQ. And individuals with higher CQ not only survive but also enjoy the invigorating challenges and insights that emerge from multicultural work. CQ will not just reduce your stress; it will also increase the personal satisfaction you experience from learning how to remain true to yourself, respect others, and collaboratively accomplish something important.

Research Note: Individuals with higher levels of CQ report a greater level of enjoyment and satisfaction from intercultural work and relationships than those with lower levels of CQ.[21]

Profitability

Finally, in light of these other benefits of CQ, it's no surprise to find a connection between CQ and profitability. Individuals who more successfully adjust cross-culturally and who perform better in fundamental tasks such as decision making, negotiations, and networking help their organizations save and earn more money. As a result, CQ increases your earning power.

One study specifically examined the role of cultural intelligence on corporate profitability. The companies involved participated in an eighteen-month cultural intelligence program that included training, hiring, and strategizing in light of CQ. Of the companies surveyed, 92 percent saw increased revenues over the eighteen-month period, all of which identified cultural intelligence as a significant contributor to their increased profits.[22]

Leading companies such as Barclays, Lloyds TSB, and Levi Strauss have all adopted cultural intelligence into their business model and have seen increased income streams, better cost management, and higher profit margins. Of course, these results aren't limited to industry giants. Small businesses, universities, charitable organizations, and government entities have seen similar gains from implementing cultural intelligence into their domestic and global operations.

Many executives see the benefits of hiring, promoting, and rewarding individuals with high CQ. On average, individuals with higher CQ earn more. Cross-cultural flexibility and an ability to negotiate with people from various cultures is a highly desirable skill set. The job market is constantly changing. It's going to become increasingly important to demonstrate cultural intelligence to secure the most sought-after positions and opportunities.[23]

Research Note: Of companies that used the cultural intelligence approach through training, hiring, and strategizing, 92 percent saw increased revenue within eighteen months of implementation. Every company named cultural intelligence as a significant factor that contributed to increased profits. Therefore, companies are prioritizing hiring and retaining personnel with high CQ.[24]

Recent research on cultural intelligence points to many promising benefits. As you increase your CQ, you can tap into one of the most important capabilities needed to thrive in today's world. Ultimately, heightened CQ helps each of us make the world a better place. Nobel Prize–winning author Elie Wiesel identifies *cultural hatred* as the major source of problems between people, across all times.[25] Cultural clashes are a major destabilizing factor in our world, whether it's neighborhood rivalries, office politics, or international disputes. Cultural intelligence provides a way to work through the many misunderstandings and conflicts that accompany cross-cultural encounters.

Ken Wilbur, a postmodern philosopher, writes, "It's not that I have to agree with everything you say, but I should attempt to at least understand it, for the opposite of mutual understanding is, quite simply, war."[26] I'm not interested in promoting a vanilla culture without all the wonderful zigzags of our colorful world. But cultural intelligence can help us replace divisive rancor with recognition, respect, and mutual understanding—the CQ difference that matters most.

CQ rests in something bigger than us. If more power, wealth, and personal success are all that drive us, we'll quickly face burnout. But as we fit into things larger than us, join them, and serve them, we can take our role in the big picture and find ourselves with heightened energy for persevering through the hard work of cross-cultural interactions. Life is about things that transcend us.[27]

MOVING FORWARD

Our lives depend on our ability to get along. Cross-cultural inter-actions are no longer the exclusive domain of Peace Corps work-ers, anthropologists, missionaries, and State Department diplo-mats. We find ourselves encountering people from vastly different cultural backgrounds. As a result, cultural clashes and the ability to effectively respect each other and work together is one of the seminal issues of our day.

Research demonstrates that individuals and organizations with higher levels of cultural intelligence are finding a better way. Enhanced CQ is proven to strengthen your ability to work effec-tively and respectfully with individuals and situations in various cultural contexts. Not only do individuals with high cultural intel-ligence survive the twists and turns of our rapidly globalizing world, they thrive in them.

Everywhere is now part of everywhere. The world is global. There's no going back. As you commit to increasing your cultural intelligence, you can join a community of individuals who are experiencing the benefits of the CQ difference.

CHAPTER 2

RESEARCH BRIEF

Twenty years ago, researchers confirmed what many business leaders had thought for a long time: A high IQ doesn't guarantee successful performance in business. You also need the skills that come from emotional and social intelligence. In fact, many CEOs used this research as fodder to tell business schools, "Quit sending us 4.0 MBA graduates who fail miserably because they have zero social skills and can't solve real problems!" Successful business requires a good dose of common sense and an ability to relate well with a lot of different people.

As a result of this research, emotional intelligence, or EQ, suddenly became the craze. Leaders in all kinds of organizations were seeing the dividends gained by enhancing the EQ of themselves and others. More recently, the same kinds of results are emerging for individuals and corporations that are embracing CQ. Some have argued that cultural intelligence is the single greatest difference between professionals who thrive in today's rapidly changing world and those who become obsolete. The social skills and common sense learned through emotional intelligence don't automatically translate into successful performance when applied to other cultures. For example, the very thing that lightens up a tense meeting or builds confidence can have the reverse impact in another cultural context. Cultural intelligence picks up where emotional intelligence leaves off. It guides leaders and their teams through the twists and turns of our frenetic, globalized economy.

As stated earlier, cultural intelligence isn't just a new and improved label for cultural competence. It's a different way of approaching the multicultural challenges and opportunities of today's world, and it's rooted in research across dozens of countries around the world. This chapter will provide a brief introduction to the research underlying the cultural intelligence difference.

IN THE BEGINNING

The driving question behind the cultural intelligence research is this: *Why can some individuals and organizations move in and out of varied cultures easily and effectively while others can't?* This is a question that has long interested researchers across a variety of academic subjects. A great deal of this long-standing research has informed my own understanding about cross-cultural effectiveness. For example, I regularly draw on the seminal contributions of Milton Bennett's work on identity and intercultural development and Hall, Hofstede, Schwartz, and Trompenaars's work on cultural dimensions.[1] One of the challenges, however, is the disconnectedness between the many different intercultural models and assessments. How do we pick between them, and how do they relate to each other?

As a whole, the intercultural field has suffered from what some academics have called the "jingle and jangle" fallacy—where evidence-based perspectives get mixed together with people's personal observations, and where learned capabilities get muddled with inherent personality traits.[2] Without an overarching research-based framework, there's little agreement about how to actually assess and enhance cultural competence. Therefore, the validity of the corresponding assessments and interventions becomes highly suspect.[3] Furthermore, most intercultural approaches focus on comparative knowledge wherein it's assumed that teaching individuals the differences between French people and Thai people will translate into an ability to work effectively with French and Thai people. It's just not that simple. Cultural knowledge and global consciousness by themselves don't translate into intercultural adaptability and successful results. A more holistic approach is required.

Soon Ang from Nanyang Technological University in Singapore is one of the pioneering researchers of cultural intelligence. Ang began to seriously consider the question of intercultural effectiveness and adaptability in the midst of consulting with companies preparing for Y2K—the ticking time bomb that had everyone anxious about what would happen when the world's computers crossed from 1999 into 2000. In 1997, Professor Ang was consulting with several companies to draw together some of the best IT professionals from around the world to help solve the much-feared technological meltdown. Early on in this work, Ang noticed that the programmers from around the world were technically competent but couldn't work together.

IQ is an important predictor of job performance in the IT profession because of the complex mental processes involved in coding and programming. And IT specialists' technical expertise in writing code is a crucial part of their success. But even though companies were putting their smartest, most technically competent performers on the Y2K project, there was an unusual level of inconsistency in what was getting accomplished by various employees. Indians and Filipinos would agree to a programming approach but then go off and code things differently. The company pulled together their brightest and best IT talent, but far too little was getting accomplished, and the clock was ticking . . . literally!

Some companies attempted to deal with the challenges being faced by doing training on work styles, emotional intelligence, and social intelligence. This approach appeared to help a little but the struggles were still significant. Emotional and practical intelligence helped the IT specialists solve problems in their own cultures, but that did not automatically translate to what they could do in unfamiliar cultural situations or with colleagues from different cultures.

As a result of this growing challenge that was facing Ang and her clients, she began to work with fellow researcher Christopher Earley to conceive of a new workplace capability—one that would eventually become CQ.

Surveying Intercultural Research

The process began by studying the most important intercultural theories and models, including those by Hall, Hofstede, Schwartz, and Trompenaars. Most of these approaches focus on enhancing one's knowledge about cultural differences, such as knowing how most Germans view time and trust building, as compared to most Japanese. But just because you understand the differences between Japanese and German cultures doesn't mean you'll actually be able to work effectively with individuals from those backgrounds. And increasingly, we encounter individuals like my friend Arthur, who has a Japanese mother and a British father and attended a Dutch school while growing up in Indonesia. What culture should I study to understand Arthur? The existing approaches don't adequately equip us to engage with these complexities that are increasingly the new normal. Something more was needed to address the problems being faced in the multicultural workplace.

Surveying Intelligence Research

In addition, the intelligence research was examined to understand its relevance to the intercultural work and relationships. It's important to understand what they were looking at here as it relates to intelligence. When you walk through your local bookstore, you can see the term *intelligence* applied to all kinds of ideas. We have books about financial intelligence, business intelligence, artistic intelligence—the list keeps going. Most of these are simply using the term *intelligence* as a creative way to talk about a particular topic, but many have little, if any, connection to the technical definition of intelligence—mental, motivational, and behavioral capabilities to understand and adapt effectively to varied situations and environments.

The most traditional way of understanding the technical idea of intelligence is IQ, measuring an individual's cognitive capabilities. But there also has been extensive scholarship on varied forms of intelligence that go beyond the traditional, academic notions of IQ.

After IQ, emotional intelligence is the form of intelligence that's most familiar to many of us. Emotional intelligence is the ability to detect and regulate the emotions of one's self and others.[4] Significant work also has been done on *social intelligence* and *practical intelligence*. Social intelligence is the ability to understand and manage other people. It's knowing how to act appropriately in social interactions.[5] Practical intelligence is the ability to solve practical problems as opposed to academic, theoretical ones.[6] All three of these intelligences—emotional, social, and practical—predict the likelihood of our effectiveness when working and relating in cultures like our own. Researchers saw the relevance of these intelligences to effective job performance, but they believed something additional was needed to address the increasing cultural complexities facing most individuals and their organizations.

Cultural Intelligence Is Born!

Researchers' extensive review of intercultural theory and intelligence approaches led to the initial conceptualization of cultural intelligence—an intelligence rooted in the same fundamentals as other intelligences but with a focus specifically on the skills needed to be effective in our globalized, interconnected world. Cultural intelligence complements these other forms of intelligence and explains why some individuals are more effective than others in culturally diverse situations. Because the norms for social interaction vary from culture to culture, it is unlikely that emotional and social intelligence will translate automatically into effective cross-cultural adjustment, interaction, and effectiveness. Likewise, because the practical challenges faced cross-culturally are related to regional and cultural factors, high scores in practical intelligence aren't a sure predictor of practical success in a new cultural context.

The first publication of cultural intelligence research was in Earley and Ang's 2003 book *Cultural Intelligence: Individual Interactions Across Cultures.*[7] They wrote the book for an academic audience. A year later, a report in the *Harvard Business Review* described cultural intelligence as a core capability essential for success in twenty-first-century business. Since then, cultural intelligence has attracted worldwide attention across diverse disciplines and has been cited in more than seventy academic journals. Most of the research has examined what gives rise to cultural intelligence and testing interventions that enhance CQ.

A variety of publications exist about cultural intelligence, many of which offer helpful insights on the challenges of working cross-culturally. But similar to other books that use the "intelligence" label liberally, some of the books and articles on *cultural intelligence* present models that have no direct correlation to the academic research on varied forms of intelligence. *Intelligence* is a label some of these authors have added to their own conceptualizations of cultural competence. There's certainly value to what many of these books have to offer. It's simply important to understand that the term *cultural intelligence* is not used consistently by all who write about it.

In contrast, Earley, Ang, and their collaborators were specifically interested in viewing cross-cultural capabilities as a form of intelligence, drawing on Sternberg and Detterman's extensive survey of intelligence research.[8] This distinction is important for a few reasons:

* Intelligence research focuses on *learned capabilities* (something you can develop through experience and learning) rather than on personality traits (something you can't change because it's hardwired into who you are).

* Intelligence research integrates a wide range of research findings from both *psychology and sociology*. Your intercultural relationships are shaped by both your individual personality and your sociocultural background. Emphasizing one without the other is limiting.

* Intelligence frameworks emphasize the capability to *reformulate one's concept of self and others* rather than just learning about cultural thinking and behavior.

* Rooting multicultural behavior in the intelligence research allows for a direct correlation with the other insights that have come from intelligence research (IQ, EQ, etc.).

Early into the emergence of CQ, I was in the midst of my own research, which was primarily focused on studying the itinerant travels of North American students and professionals going overseas for one or two weeks. My research revealed an ongoing gap in the travelers' ability to adjust to the cultural norms they encountered. Yet most of these travelers had been through cross-cultural training and they espoused a desire to be culturally aware. I was intrigued about why their training and good intentions didn't translate into effective adjustment cross-culturally. I wasn't content to merely be one more person talking about "ugly Americans" without offering a solution.

But the intercultural approaches I reviewed seemed unrealistic. They were developed for individuals who would be spending extensive time living and working abroad. The approaches focused on learning a new language and understanding the intricacies of a particular culture inside and out. I celebrate the importance of this kind of approach when it's possible, but I knew most of the travelers I had observed simply didn't have the time or the capacity for that level of preparation. Furthermore, many of them, like most of us in today's world, move in and out of countless cultural situations almost daily. So I desperately needed a different kind of solution.

A mutual colleague introduced me to Soon Ang, and I was immediately drawn to her work on CQ. As I began to study her initial findings, I knew this was a research process I was interested in joining. The prospects were extremely bright for using CQ to help the kinds of individuals I felt called to serve. I'm privileged to have encountered the cultural intelligence research during some of its earliest forms, and am grateful to be part of a global research community committed to moving the research and practice of cultural intelligence forward.

Why These Four Capabilities?

One of the consistent threads across the varied forms of intelligence is a set of four complementary factors. These four factors are consistent whether we're talking about emotional, social, practical, or cultural intelligence. The four factors are motivation, cognition, meta-cognition, and behavior.[9] These four factors are interrelated, whatever the form of intelligence. A person who knows (cognition) how to relate interpersonally but has no desire to do so (motivation) won't function in a socially intelligent way. An individual who can analyze (meta-cognition) a practical situation deeply but can't actually solve it in real life (behavior) doesn't have much practical intelligence.

In parallel fashion, cultural intelligence is a four-factor capability that consists of these same four intelligence factors—motivation, cognition, meta-cognition, and behavior. The four CQ capabilities covered in this book—CQ Drive (motivation), CQ Knowledge (cognition), CQ Strategy (meta-cognition), and CQ Action (behavior)—aren't just four ideas I decided to include based on my experience or insight. They stem from theoretically grounded scholarship on intelligence. As a result, many of the strategies included in the following chapters will not only enhance your cultural intelligence but can also strengthen your intelligence in other areas as well.

HOW IS CQ MEASURED?

Once the four-factor framework for CQ was developed, the next step was to obtain input from other academics in business, psychology, sociology, education, and anthropology to develop a valid way of assessing CQ. The question at hand was this: *Can you actually quantify an individual's capabilities for multicultural effectiveness?* The Cultural Intelligence Scale (CQS) measures an individual's competency in each of the four capabilities.[10] The empirical evidence for using the CQS as a valid measurement of intercultural capabilities was published in 2007.[11]

Although it's difficult to quantify something as subjective as intercultural capability, the CQS has amazing consistency across varied times, samples, cultures, and professions. The CQS has excellent reliabilities (all exceeded 0.70) and incremental as well as predictive validity. The CQ assessments resulting from the CQS are now being used widely by leaders in business, government, charitable settings, and universities.

The online *CQ Self-Assessment* that comes with this book is based on the CQS. It gives you a snapshot of where your greatest strengths and weaknesses lie in regard to cultural intelligence. Obviously, it's only as valid as the honesty of your responses. The goal is not to see how high you can score. Use it as a personal development tool to find out which of the four areas are strongest and weakest for you. Then you can narrow your attention on leveraging your strengths and managing your weaker areas.

The Cultural Intelligence Center also offers a *CQ Multi-Rater Assessment* (360°) that combines your self-assessment with feedback from others. In addition to personally evaluating your CQ, your colleagues or peers answer similar questions on your behalf. The *CQ Multi-Rater Assessment* provides a more complete and reliable picture of your CQ because it allows you to compare your own assessment of your CQ with how others see you. Several Fortune 500 companies, government agencies, charitable organizations, and universities are using the *CQ Multi-Rater Assessment* in their leadership development initiatives.

In addition to using these online assessments, you also can roughly gage your own CQ by simply making observations with these four capabilities in mind. As you look at your interactions cross-culturally, ask yourself about your motivation (CQ Drive), understanding (CQ Knowledge), level of awareness/ability to plan (CQ Strategy), and behavior (CQ Action).

You can also use the four CQ capabilities to roughly assess the CQ of others. Which of the four capabilities are their greatest strengths? What appear to be the areas where they need the most growth? As you watch and interact with others, you begin to see which capabilities are strongest and weakest and how that compares with other people with whom you interact.

More forms of CQ assessment are being tested, including ways to track your visual and neurological responses to various cultural situations and images. And dozens of other studies of CQ are under way at universities around the world.

MOVING FORWARD

The research on cultural intelligence is far from over. Much more needs to be studied to understand CQ and its implications for all of us. Faculty, students, and industry leaders from many countries are working together to learn how CQ can best be applied. To date, the majority of CQ research has focused on assessing and developing CQ in individuals. But more recent research is examining how to assess and develop CQ in teams and social networks. Can a company have a cumulative CQ score? What about a faith community? Do certain cities and regions display a different level of CQ than others? These are some of the facinating questions being examined.

A growing community of researchers and practitioners from around the world is working together to continue the research and application of CQ. CQ doesn't belong to any single individual or organization. It can't. The needs for cultural intelligence are too great. By reading this book, you're part of that movement. And when you take the CQ assessment, you're contributing to the next phase of CQ research because your results are anonymously kept and aggregated with those of other individuals around the world as part of the worldwide CQ norms. Most of all, when you apply these findings to your relationships and work, one by one, we can use the CQ difference to make our world a better place to live and work.

Cultural Intelligence vs. Other Intercultural Approaches

CQ differs from other leading approaches to cultural competence and intercultural interaction in five primary ways:

1. *CQ is an evidence-based meta-model for diversity and international work.* A key strength of the cultural intelligence concept is that it is a research-based, overarching framework that synthesizes volumes of material and perspectives on cross-cultural leadership and diversity. The CQ measure has been tested across multiple samples, times, and cultures.

2. *CQ is a form of intelligence.* Cultural intelligence is the only approach to intercultural effectiveness that is explicitly rooted in contemporary theories of intelligence. The four capabilities of CQ are directly connected to the four dimensions of intelligence (motivational, cognitive, meta-cognitive, and behavioral) that have been broadly researched and applied around the world. CQ is a specific form of intelligence that helps individuals to function effectively in multicultural situations.[12]

3. *CQ is more than just knowledge.* The cultural intelligence approach goes beyond simply emphasizing cultural understanding. Understanding the sociological differences in cultural beliefs, values, and behaviors is essential, but it's incomplete apart from also exploring the social-psychological dynamics involved as one person interacts with another.

4. *CQ emphasizes learned capabilities more than personality traits.* Although it's helpful to understand how our predisposed personality influences our cross-cultural behavior (e.g., extroverts vs. introverts), it can be

paralyzing because personality is difficult to change. The emphasis of CQ, however, is on what any individual can do to *enhance* cultural intelligence through education, training, and experience. CQ is not fixed. It can develop and grow, and it incorporates both individual and cultural factors of how you relate and work across cultures.

5. *CQ is not culture-specific.* Cultural intelligence is not specific to a particular culture. The emphasis is not on mastering all the specific information and behavior needed for effectiveness in individual cultures. Instead, CQ focuses on developing an overall repertoire of understanding, skills, and behaviors for making sense of the barrage of cultures we encounter daily.[13]

TAKING THE
CQ SELF-ASSESSMENT

Now it's time to assess your CQ. This will help you learn where your greatest strengths and weaknesses lie in CQ.

COMPLETE THE *CQ SELF-ASSESSMENT*

With the purchase of this book, you obtain access for one person to complete the *CQ Self-Assessment*. Locate the unique access code at the back of the book and then go to www.cqdifference.com and follow the instructions carefully.

BEFORE YOU BEGIN

Here are a few rules of thumb I've learned from using this assessment with thousands of people around the world:

- *Don't overthink your responses.* Just answer as honestly and frankly as you can. Usually, the first response that comes to mind will be the most accurate for revealing your CQ.

- *This isn't a test. You can't fail.* We're all stronger in some of the four capabilities than others. You're the only one who will see your results. The key is to find areas of strength and areas of weakness so you know where to channel your attention to gain the benefits of a heightened overall CQ.

- *You're smart.* You can game some parts of the self-assessment by figuring out how to get high scores. But then you'll miss out on the insights offered by honestly looking at where to focus your work. Be true to yourself to gain the most from this.

INTERPRETING THE RESULTS

Try not to be defensive if you aren't pleased with your scores. This is just a snapshot in time, and it's based on your frame of mind as you completed the assessment. At the same time, don't too quickly dismiss the results just because you might not agree. The assessment has been tested and validated with thousands of people across numerous life spans and cultures. The results offer some important insights for you.

Scores for the Four CQ Capabilities

You'll see several scores, the most important of which are the overall scores you received for each of the four capabilities. Enter your scores in the shaded column in the table:

1. CQ Drive (Motivation)		Your level of interest, drive, and confidence to adapt to multicultural situations
2. CQ Knowledge (Cognition)		Your level of understanding about how cultures are similar and different
3. CQ Strategy (Meta-cognition)		Your level of awareness and ability to plan for multicultural interactions
4. CQ Action (Behavior)		Your level of adaptability when relating and working cross-culturally

Are you surprised by the results? Why or why not? When you read Part II of the book, pay special attention to the strategies that go with the CQ capability where you scored lowest.

The "Low, Medium, High" ratings are based on how you evaluated yourself compared to thousands of others who have completed the assessment. This gives you some standard by which to compare your results.

Scores for the Sub-Dimensions

You'll also see several scores that are called sub-dimensions. Each of the four CQ capabilities can be further assessed and developed by paying attention to these sub-dimensions. As we walk through each of the next four chapters, we'll revisit your sub-dimension scores to help focus your attention on the strategies that may be of greatest help and interest to you for improving your CQ.

* * *

Now that you've completed the *CQ Self-Assessment,* we're ready to focus on improving your CQ. Keep your feedback report nearby to gain the most from what follows.

PART II

STRATEGIES TO IMPROVE YOUR CQ

The next four chapters are devoted to helping you improve in each of the four capabilities of CQ. You may want to read straight through this section, or it might be more helpful for you to just read the introductory material for each chapter and then focus on the list of strategies that accompany the capability where you want to begin work. Then you can come back to another list of strategies when you're ready to work on a different capability. Do what helps you most.

Several of the strategies that enhance CQ stem from things you already do in other parts of your life (e.g., setting goals, creating space for physical and emotional health, making checklists). Becoming more culturally intelligent doesn't mean you have to take on a whole new set of responsibilities. But it does require some intentionality to use these tools to strengthen your cross-cultural effectiveness. These strategies have been researched and tested academically.

There's also a story running through these chapters to demonstrate how CQ or the lack thereof shows up in real life. Like all of us, the characters demonstrate some strengths and weaknesses in their cross-cultural perspectives and interactions. I'll offer some commentary along the way about how the four CQ capabilities relate to the various individuals and events in the narrative.

CHAPTER **3**

CQ DRIVE

Cross-cultural training is usually the de-facto response for dealing with the challenges of multicultural work. As valuable as it can be to learn about cultural issues, it's ineffective without ample drive and motivation to pursue the hard work of cross-cultural effectiveness. CQ Drive asks the question: *Do you have the confidence and motivation to work through the challenges and conflict that inevitably accompany cross-cultural situations?* This is one of the most significant yet overlooked ingredients to successful work cross-culturally.

CQ Drive: The extent to which you're energized and persistent in your approach to culturally diverse situations. It includes your sense of self-confidence in your abilities as well as your sense of the rewards—both tangible and intangible—that you will gain from functioning effectively in situations characterized by cultural diversity.

Key Question: What's my level of confidence and motivation for this cross-cultural situation? If it's lacking, what can I do to increase it?

Robert, an African American CFO at an Indianapolis telecom company, is no stranger to cross-cultural issues. His extended family still marvels that he broke through the glass ceiling. He rose quickly to a C-level suite in the corporate world. He met his wife, Ingrid, a German woman from Munich, when they both attended the University of Chicago. Robert and Ingrid are a ridiculously good-looking couple with three beautiful kids. At 6'2", Robert towers above Ingrid, but she outran him last month at their local 10K race. They moved to Indiana after college when Ingrid got a job teaching German at an Indianapolis high school. Now she's the principal. Twenty years later, Indianapolis feels like home to Robert, Ingrid, and their family.

Robert spends evenings and weekends at his kids' ball games around affluent Indianapolis suburbs. He feels more at home these days among his neighbors and friends in Indianapolis than he does when he goes back to the south side of Chicago to visit his family. In fact, he finds it harder and harder to take the time to get up to Chicago to see everyone.

It's Friday morning, and Robert's day is booked solid with meetings. After his early-morning workout, the first thing he does at the office this morning is talk with his daughter Sarah on Skype. Sarah just started a study-abroad program in Budapest for the semester. This morning, she tells her dad that a group of her American friends are planning to go to T.G.I. Friday's together for dinner tonight. She's trying to convince the group to try an authentic Hungarian place instead. But a couple of her friends say they just need to eat something "normal." Besides, her roommate is freaked out to go to a Hungarian place all by themselves. At least they'll know what they're ordering at Friday's, and the servers will speak English.

While Robert listens to Sarah, he simultaneously reads through some of his e-mail that came in overnight. He says to Sarah, "Ah—lighten up, honey. They just want a good burger. There's nothing wrong with that."

Robert has several appointments this morning, and the first three are interviews for a new administrative assistant he needs to hire. Last time he needed to hire an administrative assistant, he just let human resources find the person and they hired a guy. He tries to be open-minded, but even in the twenty-first century, there's something that just seems wrong about a man being his secretary.

The first interview is with Sana, a tall, olive-skinned young woman who recently moved to Indianapolis with her husband. Sana wears a head covering to the interview. She appears to be a Muslim. She's very articulate with an impressive résumé, but Robert feels unnerved by her. He's uncertain of how Sana will fit in with the company culture. He has a hard time imagining working with a Muslim woman every day, but he knows he can't verbalize *that* to human resources.

Why isn't this easier? Robert has been looking forward to just having a competent employee who would get the job done. Ingrid's administrative assistant is a mom who has lived in Indiana her whole life. She's been working for Ingrid for eight years. Why can't human resources find someone like that for Robert?

Robert interviews two more women for the opening, and then he has five minutes to spare before today's most important appointment: a meeting with three executives from a telecom company based in the Middle East. They're interested in buying one of the best-performing business units in Robert's company. Robert has been telling his CEO he thinks they should seriously consider any fair offer.

WHAT'S CQ DRIVE GOT TO DO WITH IT?

CQ Drive is your *interest and confidence in functioning effectively in culturally diverse settings*. This often gets overlooked when dealing with issues like cultural diversity and international travel. The tendency is to immediately jump in with training (CQ Knowledge) to help people deal with cultural differences. But without the ample drive to take on the challenges that inevitably accompany multicultural situations, you're likely to experience a high rate of failure and frustration through training alone.

There are several indicators of Robert's CQ Drive in just this brief snapshot, from his reluctance to travel back home to the south side of Chicago to his interactions with his daughter and his assumptions about what would make a good administrative assistant. We'll refer back to issues like these as we walk through the strategies for enhancing our motivation for cross-cultural effectiveness.

Again, CQ Drive asks the question: *Do you have the confidence and drive to work through the challenges and conflict that inevitably accompany cross-cultural situations?* The ability to be personally engaged and persevere through cross-cultural challenges is one of the most novel and important aspects of cultural intelligence. Study-abroad students are often more interested in the adventure of a semester overseas, hitting the pubs, and fulfilling their academic requirements than they are in interacting with the local culture. Employees often approach diversity training apathetically, and do it just because it's required. Personnel headed to international assignments are often more concerned about moving and adjusting their families overseas than they are about developing cultural understanding.

High CQ Drive stems from an intrinsic interest in a different culture and a confidence to be able to relate effectively and naturally in that culture. The Hungarian culture probably doesn't seem nearly as foreign to Sarah as it does to her American friends because of her mom's German roots. Individuals with high CQ

Drive are motivated to learn and adapt to new and diverse cultural settings. Their confidence in their adaptive abilities is likely to influence the way they act in multicultural situations.

If you have high CQ Drive, you might become easily frustrated with others who don't share your cross-cultural curiosities and interests. You tell them about an overseas adventure or about a new ethnic restaurant you discovered and they give you a blank stare. Keep in mind that not everyone is equally energized by all things cross-cultural—and that's okay.

ASSESSING YOUR CQ DRIVE

How is your CQ Drive? Are you motivated to discover new cultures and confident you can engage effectively when you work and relate cross-culturally? Based on the feedback report that accompanies the online *CQ Self-Assessment*, what overall CQ Drive score did you receive?

Overall CQ Drive:_____
Did you rate yourself low, medium, or high compared
to others who have completed the *CQ Self-Assessment*?
(circle one)

Low   Medium   High

From what you're learning about CQ Drive in this chapter, are you surprised by the results? Keep in mind that the self-assessment is just one snapshot of your view of your CQ capabilities at a particular point in time. But it's worth considering the results, given the high level of reliability found in the assessment as it is used among individuals around the world.

In order to dig more deeply into your CQ Drive, the *CQ Self-Assessment* also helps you assess your motivation for multicultural situations in three specific areas of CQ Drive (intrinsic, extrinsic, and self-efficacy). There has been extensive research examining the way these various bases of motivation influence your overall drive and perseverance through the hard work of multicultural interactions.[1] Write your scores for each of the following and note the descriptions of these sub-dimensions.

Intrinsic: _____

> This is the extent to which you demonstrate a natural interest and enjoyment in multicultural experiences.
> A high score means you're energized and enthused by the chance to explore different cultures. A low score means you don't derive enjoyment from culturally diverse experiences in and of themselves.

Extrinsic: _____

> This is the extent to which you see tangible benefits from multicultural interactions and experiences. A high score means you think multicultural work helps build respect and accelerate success in your career or other pursuits. A low score means you don't give much thought to the external benefits of multicultural experiences.

Self-Efficacy: _____

> This is your level of confidence in doing cross-cultural work effectively. A high score means you expect to succeed in a cross-cultural encounter, and a low score means you're uncertain and maybe even anxious about how you will behave in multicultural situations.

These three sub-dimensions of CQ Drive—intrinsic, extrinsic, and self-efficacy—are the scientific bases for the strategies that follow. You'll see these sub-dimensions alongside the list of strategies at the beginning of the next section. Not every strategy fits perfectly with a single sub-dimension, but the strategies have been organized according to the sub-dimension with which they are most closely associated. Use your scores from the sub-dimensions of CQ Drive to help you pinpoint which strategies to use first (presumably, the strategies that go with the sub-dimension where you scored lowest).

DRIVE

IMPROVING YOUR CQ DRIVE

The following section is a list of strategies to help you improve your CQ Drive. All these strategies are anchored in science and research on motivation for multicultural situations and stem from the three sub-dimensions of CQ Drive (intrinsic, extrinsic, and self-efficacy). The point is not for you to use all these strategies right now. There are many paths to increasing CQ Drive. Start with a couple that interest you.

1. Face your biases. 2. Connect with existing interests. 3. Scare yourself.	Intrinsic
4. Visualize success. 5. Reward yourself. 6. Recharge your batteries.	Extrinsic
7. Maintain control. 8. Travel.	Self-Efficacy

1. FACE YOUR BIASES

To what cultures are you naturally drawn? Which ones make you uncomfortable? It might sound noble to say we view everyone the same, but it's just not true. Whenever we meet someone, we subconsciously categorize them as a "friend" or a "foe." It does little good to deny this. Honestly explore what subcultures really push your hot buttons, set up your defenses, or just make you uncomfortable. An important strategy for enhancing CQ Drive is admitting the implicit prejudices and biases we have toward certain groups of people and working to overcome them.[2]

From the moment we're born, we're taught to see the world in a certain way. Most of this socialization process occurs subconsciously. Our parents teach us what's "normal" and what's "weird." We're quickly given a sense of right versus wrong and success versus failure. Our childhood networks expand to include extended family, neighbors, and school friends and our view of the world is developed further. But usually these individuals further reinforce what we've been learning at home. We're taught good and bad manners, what it means to be a man or woman, and how to get ahead in life. Then we watch for cues about how to act and the consequences for those who don't conform. As we continue through high school and go on to college or the working world, we continue to learn what's cool, important, and right.

Most of us feel the greatest trust and warmth when we're with people like us; we feel uncomfortable and suspicious of people who are different. Even so-called "alternative" groups usually conform to the agendas and styles of other alternatives in their subculture. There's something secure and stabilizing about being with people who view the world like us. Laughing together about things we find funny, ranting together about things that tick us off, and sharing an appreciation for some of the same food, art, and perspectives on the world can be the ingredients for building serendipitous memories together. But it also can further reinforce our biases about people who view the world differently.

We all have implicit biases. The key is whether we act on them. One way to explore your biases is through some tests developed at Harvard called *implicit association tests*. These tests expose the implicit biases we have toward people's skin color, weight, age, and religion. They're fascinating! You can find them at https://implicit.harvard.edu/implicit/. The tests reveal automatic impulses we have toward certain cultural groups. The goal is to be honest about our biases instead of pretending they don't exist. While our internal biases are automatic, honestly understanding them can help control and moderate our interactions. We can make a deliberate choice to suspend the judgment we're biased to make. Anytime you meet someone new, make an effort to connect with them on a human level as early as possible rather than just seeing them in light of their cultural context (e.g., she's a parent like me; or he is looking for a way to do something significant in his life like I am).

Think back to the opening scene with Robert and Sana. It would be helpful for Robert to stop and acknowledge his implicit bias about the kinds of jobs men should have and what it means to work closely with people from different faiths. There's also something underlying his resistance to make trips back home to the south side of Chicago. No matter how busy we are, we make time to see the people who are really important to us. The first step for Robert is to acknowledge his biases, which in and of itself can weaken their ability to determine his behavior.

Biases are inevitable. Acting on them isn't. Spend time learning what implicit prejudices you have. Notice how they influence your thoughts and behaviors. The next time you encounter someone from a culture against whom you have some implicit bias, make a deliberate choice to see the person beyond your prejudiced stereotype.

2. CONNECT WITH EXISTING INTERESTS

Think of a hobby that naturally energizes you. It can be anything—cooking, exercise, fashion, photography, music—you name it. Now think of a way to connect that interest to a cross-cultural context. Most of our interests exist in some form among a variety of cultures. This strategy takes an area where you're naturally motivated and draws from that motivation to increase your CQ Drive. Connect an existing interest to a cross-cultural situation or assignment.[3]

If you like art, what artistic expressions can you discover in a different cultural context? If you love sports, discover what sports are hot there and find a way to attend a sporting event. If you're a foodie, the options are endless. If you eat, drink, and sleep business, use the cross-cultural endeavor as a way to learn new business insights.

I love to run. And one of the first things I do when I get to a new place is look for where I can go for a run. Not only does it help me deal with jet lag, but I get to take in the sights and sounds of a different terrain. I have a different set of physical challenges when I'm running in the desert-like climate of Dubai than when I'm running through the humidity of Bangkok. Running in the city is different from running along a mountainous trail in the Alps. All of these connect one of my existing interests to places I travel. It's something I look forward to when traveling to a new place.

We have to be careful not to exploit different cultures and people simply to pursue our selfish interests. But as we factor in the other priorities of cultural intelligence, our natural interests can provide powerful connections for increasing our CQ Drive.

3. SCARE YOURSELF

There's a reason why so many politicians and marketers use fear to motivate us. Brain researchers say one of the built-in preoccupations of all humans is to minimize danger to ourselves and those we love. When you're scared, you pay attention. It makes you highly alert. Fear causes a deep and immediate alertness. Think about what happens when you're driving sleepy along a highway. If you suddenly veer onto the rumble strips on the side of the road, you immediately wake up. A similar kind of alertness happens for many people who fear public speaking. Our brains produce higher levels of adrenaline when we're afraid.[4]

Despite the popularity of fear tactics among many politicians, news pundits, and religious leaders, I'm not a big fan of using fear to motivate people. In fact, I don't like it at all unless there's a very genuine danger. But given that our safety—be it physical, psychological, vocational, or otherwise—is such a high value for us, we can find ways to use this intrinsic power of fear to our advantage when working to enhance our CQ Drive.[5]

Fortunately, you don't have to be in real danger to experience the adrenaline rush that comes from fear. Think about how your heart starts racing when you're watching a movie and an attack is about to happen. Watching a villain sneak up on an unsuspecting victim gets your heart racing. Fear makes you alert even if it's not based on reality. One way you can use fear to develop your CQ Drive is by visualizing the cost of *not* becoming more culturally intelligent. Low CQ will make you look ignorant, clueless, and self-absorbed. Worse yet, cultural ignorance can cost you your job, rob you of great opportunities, or even put your life at risk.

One time a group of Liberian educators told me about an American construction team that came to Liberia to build a school. The Liberians were extremely grateful for the team's interest and investment in helping them rebuild their country after so many years of civil war. But as the American men began to build the school, the Liberians gently suggested there would be a better kind of roof for the school that would not only be less expensive but also better able to handle the tropical weather in the region. The builders scoffed at the "ignorant," unsolicited input from the Liberians and quickly let them know they've done this kind of work all over the world and this would definitely be the best way to build the school roof. Three months later, a monsoon came through, the roof came crashing down and killed some of the children inside and injured many more. Taking time to listen and heed the insights of people from different cultural backgrounds is about more than just interacting with respect and dignity. It may be a matter of life and death—yours or someone else's.

You can use the power of fear to enhance your CQ Drive. Visualize the potential career implications of cultural ignorance. Growing numbers of organizations are assessing what it costs them when employees are ineffective cross-culturally. Some of the questions they ask include the following:

• Which senior-level leaders have had to deal with the fallout from an unsuccessful cross-cultural venture? What's their pay? Try putting an hourly rate on their time and calculate the cost.

• What other staff had to get involved in this failure? How much did their time on this cost?

• What opportunities were missed because of all the energy diverted toward this issue?

Imagine being viewed as a liability when it comes to your employer's interests in cross-cultural markets. Use this fear to increase your motivation to do cross-cultural work well. Make yourself indispensable.

Sarah's roommate in Budapest feels safer when she thinks about going to T.G.I. Friday's because it's familiar. She assumes the staff will speak English, and that gives her a sense of safety. But going to an unfamiliar place with a group of friends might seem less threatening than venturing out all by herself. Perhaps her fear could motivate her to seek out some Hungarian students who could join them. Not only would she have someone along who "knew the ropes" and could speak the language, but this would also allow the American students the chance to begin interacting with locals rather than just observing them from afar. And interacting with and learning from the locals in Hungary might have as much or more to do with getting a good job when they graduate than the classes they'll attend while they're in Budapest. Think about what seems most threatening for you, and look for ways to orient those fears toward becoming more culturally intelligent.

4. VISUALIZE SUCCESS

I'm an eternal optimist, so I'm a much bigger fan of motivating ourselves and others with the possibility of opportunity and success rather than with fear. Instead of visualizing the failure that can occur if you don't become more culturally intelligent, imagine the possibilities if you do.

Think of a time when you were successful interacting with someone from a different cultural background. What can you learn from that experience? As simplistic as it might sound, just "imagining" your cross-cultural success and the corresponding benefits can powerfully influence your CQ drive. Many of the situations that are most difficult for you don't come up as often as it might seem. Picture the kind of cross-cultural situation that's most difficult for you. For example, imagine trying to negotiate pricing with a prospective client who offers you virtually no feedback. Then imagine how it could go in a way that would make you feel successful. Walk through it in your head as an imaginary scenario. Scientists have found that anticipating a positive outcome, anything the brain perceives as a forthcoming reward, actually generates energy.[6]

Make a list of the tangible benefits you can obtain by improving your CQ. We looked at several benefits that come from heightened CQ in Chapter 1 (cross-cultural adjustment, job performance, personal satisfaction, and profitability). Review these often. Visualize being your organization's best decision maker, negotiator, and networker. These are realistic prospects with increased CQ, and bearing this in mind can be a powerful source of motivation.

By improving your CQ and hence the effectiveness of your multicultural capabilities, you increase the probability of:

• Landing your dream job

• Gaining a competitive edge as an innovator

- Developing friendships with new and diverse people

- Becoming a leading activist for a cause that's important to you

- Broadening and deepening your faith

- Earning more money to support what matters to you most

Just as we used the fear of what can come about as a result of cultural ignorance, visualize the success that awaits you with increased CQ. Even if you aren't naturally interested in all things cross-cultural, think about how pursuing the hard work of culturally intelligent engagement increases your likelihood of succeeding at something that is really important to you. You may quickly find yourself gaining an appetite for prioritizing CQ as a way to enjoy some of the opportunities awaiting you.

5. REWARD YOURSELF

Whether it's an exercise regime, breaking an addiction, or saving money, psychologists continually examine the power of rewards to modify our behavior. We use this with kids all the time. We get them to do something by promising a prize or reward. This is another strategy we can use to enhance our CQ Drive.[7]

To benefit from this strategy, first you need to set some goals for increasing your cultural intelligence. Goals orient the brain to move toward a particular end. Be sure the goals are realistic; otherwise, they can decrease your CQ Drive. Don't come up with too many.[8]

Now create some rewards for reaching your goals. Without any rewards, you'll be tempted to abandon the perseverance needed to improve your CQ. Don't just reward yourself for big accomplishments; reward small steps as well. If your goal is to learn five phrases in a different language, then reward yourself as soon as you can recall each one.

It's ideal if the reward somewhat correlates to the goal itself (e.g., learning Spanish and then going out for a Mexican meal where you order in Spanish). But even if the reward isn't directly related to the goal, rewarding yourself for reaching goals is a strong way to increase your motivation. Give yourself something that will reinforce the behavior for the next time. Rewards can be as simple as watching your favorite TV show, buying your favorite food, or even just taking a few minutes to sit back and veg out. It needs to be something you wouldn't have otherwise done or you aren't training yourself for this particular behavior.

The most important time to reward yourself is immediately after doing the particular task you set out to do. Associating good feelings with the practice and application of the skill will bring your entire mind into the learning process required for enhanced CQ. You can experiment with different rewards to see what works best for you.

Eventually something deeper, intrinsic, and more transcendent needs to drive us. In fact, cultural intelligence cannot exist apart from true love for the world and for people.[9] At the very core of cultural intelligence is the desire to learn with and about other people. So our drive will need to go beyond the rewards we give ourselves. But as we fit into things larger than us, join them, and serve them, rewarding ourselves along the way can be a helpful way to help us persevere.

6. RECHARGE YOUR BATTERIES

Cross-cultural interaction and work is fatiguing. Even people with high CQ are more quickly drained by working and relating cross-culturally than when doing so in familiar contexts. It's likely that it's going to require more energy for Robert to interview Sana than for him to interview someone more similar to himself. There's a heightened level of energy and focus required to keep up with cross-cultural demands and challenges. When you're in the midst of cross-cultural situations, find ways to recharge your batteries. Otherwise, if you associate your cross-cultural interactions and work with exhaustion and fatigue, your CQ Drive will suffer. Our bodies and psyche are wired for health and replenishment.

There are lots of resources available to help us recharge our batteries amidst our frenzied lives, many of which can help us enhance our CQ Drive. Your physical and mental well-being are directly connected to your CQ Drive. Perhaps the best thing you can do to enhance your CQ Drive is to take a nap. Sleep, exercise, and healthy eating are one of the ways to increase your energy level. Go for a good run, drink some coffee (or your preferred beverage), and leave some margin for recreation. Play a round of golf or spend time with your partner or a friend. For some of us, an unscheduled day at home is the best way to recharge, while others of us will be energized by a hard workout and a busy day with friends. Taking time to care for your physical and mental health has implications on so many fronts, one of which is your ability to be effective and resilient cross-culturally.

The importance of your health and stamina to your CQ Drive is greatest when your cross-cultural activity involves international travel. The hard work of cross-cultural interaction becomes compounded when we're dealing with jet lag and being away from home. Dealing with jet leg is more an art than a science. You can find lots of recommended techniques online such as setting your watch to the time at your destination as soon as you board the plane; not taking afternoon naps; getting a lot of sunshine; exercising first thing in the morning, and so on. You'll learn what works best for you. Don't shrug off the importance of your physical stamina to how you work and relate cross-culturally. Your CQ Drive is affected by your physical and mental energy.

I'm a strong advocate for eating local food when traveling and in immersing myself in whatever culture I encounter. But when traveling for several days in an unfamiliar place, there's something to be said for eating something that's more familiar for an occasional meal. If you typically eat Indian food, grabbing a curried meal somewhere can help you recharge before going back to just eating the local fare. If you're a Starbucks addict, a quick fix can give you just the recharge you need.

Another way to recharge your batteries is to deliberately disconnect from your tech gadgets. The "always-connected" capability afforded us through smart phones is wearing us out and may actually be making us dumber. One University of London study found that individuals who are constantly connected via e-mail, texting, and social networking sites experienced a ten-point drop in their IQ. In fact, researchers found that constantly being "on" via technology has a similar effect to regularly giving up one night of sleep. The problem isn't using technology. That's a no-brainer for most of us in today's world. The problem is what it does to our mental health when we never unplug from the distractions of technological connectivity.[10]

Choose specific times to connect technologically and then shut it off so your brain can focus more deeply. This will have implications that go far beyond CQ Drive, but it's one of the simple strategies you can employ that will allow you to channel the increased energy that ensues toward your cross-cultural work.

Before we're too quick to criticize Robert for reading his e-mail while talking to his daughter overseas, how many of us do the same thing all the time? And for those of us who pride ourselves on being able to multitask, research demonstrates we can't really focus deeply on multiple things at the same time, no matter who you are. Robert can't really engage with his daughter and her cross-cultural issues with her friends while also tending to his e-mail.

Things as simple as taking a brisk walk, closing your e-mail program, and getting a full night of sleep can increase your CQ Drive. Maybe you need to close this book and go take a nap.

7. MAINTAIN CONTROL

Most cross-cultural training emphasizes the importance of flexibility and going with the flow. I wholeheartedly agree with the importance of flexibility. But sometimes we take this ideal too far and presume it means we shouldn't plan or try to control anything that happens in a cross-cultural situation. Sometimes we use "flexibility" as an excuse for laziness and lack of planning. CQ Drive is enhanced when we have a sense of autonomy, which is directly connected to the level of control we feel over our circumstances.[11]

Evidence indicates all humans and animals are threatened by a loss of control. Amy Arnsten, a neurobiologist at Yale University, studies the effects of feeling in control upon how we function. The brain actually functions less efficiently when we believe we're out of control. In contrast, even an illusion of control helps the brain perform more optimally. The perception of being in control is a major driver of behavior.[12]

Stress is most damaging when it results from something unexpected and when we feel like there's no way we can stop it. We feel out of control when we lose a job or, worse yet, a loved one and as a result, the stress can be debilitating. However, when stress is self-induced, such as the stress from a new exercise regime or from pursuing a graduate degree, the stress can actually be a motivator because it's something we chose to inflict upon ourselves.

We see the way gaining control motivates people who leave the stability of a job to start their own businesses. Many individuals do so because they're sick of the crazy demands placed on them by employers. Yet these entrepreneurs usually work more hours, for less money, than they ever did working for someone else. But as business owners, they're able to make their own choices and, as a result, they have a higher degree of motivation. In contrast, when you feel like you have less control—for example, because you're on an international trip where you're entirely dependent on a host to get you around and communicate—it often feels threatening.[13] Start slowly. Take a walk by yourself. Go to the store and buy a newspaper on your own. Then try public transportation on your own. These kinds of baby steps enhance your sense of control, which, in turn, increases your CQ Drive.

If we've learned anything about cross-cultural relationships and experiences, it's that they're highly unpredictable. But many things aren't as unpredictable as we might think. We can feel a greater sense of control, agency, and therefore CQ Drive by simply taking time to maintain control of our priorities while traveling. This requires a little planning ahead. If you like to run, figure out how, where, and when to work that into your schedule. If it's important to stay in touch with family or friends, a little homework can help you figure out how to make that happen in most places where you go without spending $3/minute to call home.

The need for control is especially true for those of us who come from highly individualistic cultures (i.e., most "Western" cultures) where we're used to shaping our own destiny. When you find ways to make choices, your stress is reduced. If all you can do is choose your response to an event, that kind of control is still useful. When traveling, learn how to cope for yourself so that you aren't entirely dependent on someone else. When managing and guiding others, find ways to give them choices, such as when and where to eat and how to develop a negotiation strategy. Increase your sense of control over cross-cultural situations and you'll enhance your CQ Drive.

8. TRAVEL

As you can probably guess, frequent cross-cultural experiences are a good way to enhance your CQ Drive. Multiple experiences traveling and interacting cross-culturally create an enhanced sense of familiarity, comfort, and confidence for you in future intercultural interactions.[14] Gaining direct experience working, volunteering, or studying in cross-cultural situations, watching others who do it successfully, and learning "on the job" are some of the most important ways to gain confidence to do it more.

Cross-cultural experience by itself does not ensure cultural intelligence. Just because you do something a lot doesn't necessarily mean you learn from it. But when experience and frequent travel are combined with the capabilities and priorities of cultural intelligence, it plays a significant role in enhancing our CQ Drive—particularly our confidence. Individuals with multiple experiences in different places experience more of the benefits of travel to CQ Drive than those who have only been in one or two places, even if for a long time. That's because multiple experiences in varied locations force you to keep adapting and recalibrating how you relate and work, and the more experience you have doing so, the greater your sense of confidence.

In addition, the more countries where you've lived for more than a year, the more positive connection there is between your cross-cultural experience and cultural intelligence.[15] Childhood experiences play less of a role in developing CQ if children simply accompany their parents, though surely this provides a wonderful opportunity to begin learning about the world at a young age. But as adolescents and adults make their own choices about cross-cultural travel, work, and interaction, the travel is more likely to lead to increased CQ.[16] Similar kinds of confidence-building can occur through multicultural experiences done domestically.

There are many fun, safe, and relatively inexpensive places where you can vacation or study without spending a ton of money. Scope out the local haunts, walk the streets, shop the local markets, and take in as much of the culture as you can without being a nuisance. Volunteer with a nonprofit organization doing relief work. Do a Spanish immersion program in Quito or a Mandarin immersion in Kunming. Accept work assignments that put you in contact with people from different cultural backgrounds. All these experiences contribute to increasing your CQ Drive, which will further your effectiveness in future cross-cultural experiences.[17]

Robert's daughter Sarah has traveled with her family to visit her relatives in Germany. That experience gives her more confidence to strike out and go to a local restaurant in Budapest without help from a local. She needs to realize that her friends haven't had as many opportunities to do this and look for ways to help them use their time in Budapest to make future cross-cultural experiences easier.

Robert needs to explore his implicit biases regarding gender roles and religious differences. Instead of seeing a colleague's differences as a threat, he should consider the benefits to him personally and to the company. If the company is going to effectively expand into more diverse markets, it needs the input of people like Sana, the woman Robert is interviewing. Robert could be much better prepared for a meeting with Middle Eastern executives if he had a colleague like Sana. A culturally diverse workforce enhances an organization's ability to meet the opportunities and demands of our globalized world.

As we more closely encounter Sana, we'll see ways that her CQ Drive influences her behavior as well. She recently moved away from her family network that existed in Detroit, where she and her husband lived previously. Although Indianapolis is only a few hours away, it's a very different subculture from Detroit. Her need to find a job can be as powerful a motivation as anything to help her increase her CQ Drive.

Robert's daughter Sarah should be aware that she has a different level of confidence cross-culturally than many of her peers. Rather than becoming frustrated or lording her experience in Europe over them, she can help them increase their CQ Drive by alleviating some of their fear of the unknown and help them see the benefits of encountering the local culture in Budapest.

INCREASING YOUR CQ DRIVE

Many of these motivational strategies apply to many aspects of our lives. Think about which ones to enlist to enhance your motivation and confidence for cross-cultural situations.

Identify two strategies you can begin using to enhance your CQ Drive.

❑ 1. Face your biases. ❑ 2. Connect with existing interests. ❑ 3. Scare yourself.	Intrinsic
❑ 4. Visualize success. ❑ 5. Reward yourself. ❑ 6. Recharge your batteries.	Extrinsic
❑ 7. Maintain control. ❑ 8. Travel.	Self-Efficacy

Which one will you use first? When?

CHAPTER **4**

CQ KNOWLEDGE

One of the best ways to deal with the ambiguity faced in multicultural situations is by learning more about cultural differences. Even though intercultural understanding by itself doesn't equal effectiveness, it is an essential part of alleviating the confusion that often ensues from this kind of work. CQ Knowledge asks the question: *Do you have the cultural understanding needed to be more effective cross-culturally?* Growth in CQ Knowledge can significantly strengthen your effectiveness in a myriad of areas.

CQ Knowledge: The extent to which you understand the role of culture in how people think and behave and your level of familiarity with how cultures are similar and different.

Key Question: What cultural understanding do I need to be more effective cross-culturally?

Sana was born near Detroit, Michigan. Her parents came to the United States from Yemen in the late sixties to study at the University of Michigan. Her dad got a good job, and they ended up staying. Many more of their relatives followed. Last month was the first time Sana visited Yemen herself. She and Haani took a delayed honeymoon to the Middle East and visited Haani's relatives in Jordan, then her family in Yemen, and ended with a few days by themselves in Dubai before coming home to pack up and move to Indianapolis.

Walking the streets of Sanaa and Amman, the capital cities of Yemen and Jordan, was surreal for Sana. For the first time in her life, she was surrounded by people who looked like her. She felt like she was home—sort of, anyway. In other ways, she felt like a complete outsider. Everyone seemed to make assumptions about her and Haani's wealth, religious convictions, and views on U.S. foreign policy. After so many years of being stereotyped back home for being Middle Eastern, now they were feeling stereotyped for being "American." During their last day in Yemen, all of Sana's aunts sat her down and told her she must reconsider moving away from Michigan to this new city (Indianapolis). Her aunt scolded her, "How can you and Haani leave your families like this? It's just not right, Sana. This is bringing great shame to us. You're behaving like infidels."

Infidels? Moving to Indianapolis from Detroit was very exciting for Sana and Haani. This was a chance to build a new home together. They came here because Haani was offered a two-year research fellowship with a large pharmaceutical company. Despite the small stipend, Haani knew this was a much sought-after opportunity. Sana had agreed to find a steady job to support them. She's not too worried about finding a job because she's always succeeded at whatever she set out to do. But the interviewing process is new to her. Before the move, she had worked for her father at his dental practice in Michigan. .

This morning, Sana is interviewing for an administrative assistant position at a telecom company. She's five minutes early for the interview but she has to wait a half hour before Robert, the CFO, brings her into his office. While waiting, she notices everyone is dressed casually. The receptionist says, "Gotta love casual Fridays!" Sana feels like people in Indianapolis stare at her head covering much more than they ever did in Detroit.

When Robert comes to greet her, she wonders why he's wearing a suit and tie on "casual Friday." She awkwardly shakes his hand, and he spends the first several minutes talking about his daughter, who is studying in Budapest. *Just like my dad*, she thought. *He's so proud of his daughter.*

Out of the corner of her eye, Sana sees a plaque that says, "It's not a religion. It's a relationship." Just then, Robert says, "So your résumé says you're bilingual. I must say, you do speak really great English." Then he asks, "So how long have you lived in the U.S.?" He seems taken back when she responds, "All my life."

At the end of the interview, Sana says, "My husband would like to meet you. May I give him your number?" For the first time all morning, Robert seems speechless. Finally, he responds, "Let's see how the interviewing process goes. If you're back for a second interview, we can talk about it then."

Robert has fifteen minutes before his next interview, so he pulls out the agenda for today's big meeting regarding the potential acquisition by the Middle Eastern company. In thinking about the meeting, he wonders if there's a tactful way to bring up what his friend Sharon told him last week over coffee. When Robert confidentially told Sharon they might sell one of their business lines to a successful Middle Eastern firm, Sharon said, "Just be careful. Business runs on a different set of rules over there." She told him about a time when her colleague Alvin, a Singaporean manager from her company, was sent to the Middle East to establish a new regional hub for the business.

When Alvin arrived in the Middle East from Singapore, he went straight to the immigration office to deal with the necessary permits for conducting business there. Alvin was smartly dressed for his meeting with the immigration official. He completed the application impeccably and handed over the documents and corresponding fees. But he didn't offer the official any kind of tip for getting this paperwork completed. He was confused when the officer said some additional paperwork was needed. Alvin brought everything the website said he needed and even called ahead to confirm that he was prepared.

Alvin went back two more times, and on each occasion, he became more irritated at the delays. But despite some broad hints dropped by the immigration officer, Alvin still didn't offer any cash as a personal accommodation. So the officer persisted in his approach. *If Alvin won't play the game according to the established rules, he will have to accept the consequences.*

As Robert listened to Sharon recount this experience, he said, "Well, that's just corrupt. That isn't a tip. It's a bribe."

"I know" Sharon responded. "That's what we all thought. And we all have to sign agreements with the company promising that we won't pay or accept bribes of any kind. But I guess that's just the way business is done there. Immigration officers are paid a very low wage with the assumption that the individuals served will show their appreciation with small sums of money. I'm just saying, Robert, you better know what you're getting into if you're going to do business with a company over there. They play by different rules."

But there's no time for Robert to think any more about that right now. The next applicant just arrived for her interview—a loud-spoken woman with a strong southern accent. Oh, dear Lord, Robert thinks. *Does HR do any screening before they send me these people?*

WHAT'S CQ KNOWLEDGE GOT TO DO WITH IT?

CQ Knowledge is your *understanding about culture and how it shapes behavior.* This is the area most often emphasized in cross-cultural preparation—learning about cultural values and differences. Its importance cannot be overstated. As we learn more about cultures and different ways of doing things, it helps us better understand what's going on, which, in turn, helps us relate and work more effectively.

There are so many ways enhanced CQ Knowledge could help Sana and Robert. We get a glimpse into Sana's level of cultural understanding by the way she receives the criticisms from her Yemeni aunts and the nature of her questions and comments to Robert during their interview. And Robert's conversations with Sana and his friend Sharon indicate something about his CQ Knowledge. A greater degree of CQ Knowledge will help Robert conduct a better, more effective interview, and it will help Sana be more successful in pitching herself to potential employers.

Again, CQ Knowledge asks the question: *Do you have the cultural understanding needed to be more effective cross-culturally?* The emphasis here is not on mastering all the ins and outs of each specific culture. If Robert was going to do a lot of extensive work in Yemen, he'd be wise to gain some very specialized understanding of the history, character, and cultural nuances of Yemen. But Robert can't realistically become an expert on Yemen simply for a forty-five-minute interview. The most important part of CQ Knowledge is developing a richer understanding of culture, its influence on thinking and behavior, and the primary ways cultures differ.

With high CQ Knowledge, you have a holistic, well-organized understanding of culture and how it affects the way people think and behave. It begins with a strong sense of your own cultural identity and the way the cultures of which you're part shape your behavior. When you have high CQ Knowledge, you possess a repertoire of understanding about how cultures are alike and different. You can encounter unfamiliar cultures and begin to understand a culture in light of your overall cultural understanding.[1]

ASSESSING YOUR CQ KNOWLEDGE

How is your CQ Knowledge? To what degree do you understand how cultures are similar and different? Based on the feedback report that accompanies the online *CQ Self-Assessment*, what overall CQ Knowledge score did you receive?

Overall CQ Knowledge:_____
   Did you rate yourself low, medium, or high compared
   to others who have completed the *CQ Self-Assessment*?
   (circle one)

Low   *Medium*   *High*

From what you're learning about CQ Knowledge in this chapter, are you surprised by the results? Keep in mind that the self-assessment is just one snapshot of your view of your CQ capabilities at a particular point in time. But it's worth considering the results given the high level of reliability found in the assessment as used among individuals around the world.

In order to dig more deeply into your CQ Knowledge, the inventory also helps you assess your cultural understanding in the four specific areas of CQ Knowledge (business, interpersonal, socio-linguistics, and leadership). Extensive research has examined the way these various bases of knowledge influence your overall understanding and insight as you interact cross-culturally.[2] Write your scores for each of the following and note the descriptions of these sub-dimensions.

Business (Legal and Economic Systems): _____
> This is the extent to which you understand the various cultural systems that exist in places around the world (e.g., economic, legal, educational). It's not simply for people in business, but it does refer to your knowledge of some of the different approaches used for business in various cultures. A high score means you have a good grasp of the various systems that exist among different national cultures. A low score means you have limited understanding about the varying economic and legal systems between one country and the next.

Interpersonal: _____
> This is the extent to which you know about how cultures differ in their values, norms for social etiquette, and religious perspectives. A high score means you have a strong understanding of cultural values and how they play out in various contexts. A low score means you rated yourself low in your knowledge of the norms and values of various cultures.

Socio-Linguistics: _____
> This is your understanding of different languages and your knowledge of various rules for how language gets expressed verbally and nonverbally in various cultures. A high score means you understand the rules for verbal and nonverbal behavior for many cultures and a low score means you don't.

Leadership: _____
This is your level of understanding about how effective
management differs across cultures. A high score means
you rated yourself strongly in terms of your knowledge
about managing people and relationships across cultures.
A low score means you have limited understanding of
how management and relationships differ from one
place to the next.

These four sub-dimensions of CQ Knowledge—business, interpersonal, socio-linguistics, and leadership—are the scientific bases
for the strategies that follow. You'll see these sub-dimensions alongside the list of strategies at the beginning of the next section. Not
every strategy fits perfectly with a single sub-dimension, but the
strategies have been organized according to the sub-dimension with
which they are most closely associated. Use your scores from the
sub-dimensions of CQ Knowledge to help you pinpoint which
strategies to use first (presumably, the strategies that go with the
sub-dimension where you scored lowest).

IMPROVING YOUR CQ KNOWLEDGE

The following section is a list of strategies to help you improve your CQ Knowledge. All these strategies are anchored in science and research on intercultural knowledge and stem from the four sub-dimensions of CQ Knowledge (business, interpersonal, socio-linguistics, and leadership). The point is not for you to use all these strategies right now. There are many paths to increasing CQ Knowledge. Start with a couple that interest you.

1. Study culture up close. 2. Google smarter. 3. Improve your global awareness.	Business/Cultural Systems
4. Go to the movies or read a novel. 5. Learn about cultural values. 6. Explore your cultural identity.	Interpersonal/Cultural Values
7. Study a new language.	Socio-Linguistics
8. Seek diverse perspectives. 9. Recruit a CQ coach.	Leadership

KNOWLEDGE

1. STUDY CULTURE UP CLOSE

There's no better way to learn about culture than when you're in it. Culture is all around us and influences everyone and everything. But it's easy to miss it if we don't intentionally look for it. Adolescent researcher Terry Linhart traveled with a group of U.S. high school students to Ecuador to observe how they interacted with the local culture during their two-week trip there. He said their interaction with the Ecuadoreans was similar to how people act when they visit a museum. The students gawked at the "living artifacts" from Ecuador without really encountering them. The high schoolers performed for the Ecuadoreans, poured out affection on the children, and visited local businesses. However, with limited ability to understand the culture, and even less ability to speak Spanish, the students were unable to make accurate perceptions about the locals they encountered. Linhart writes, "Without spending significant time with the person, visiting his or her home, or even possessing rudimentary knowledge about the person's history, students made quick assessments of their hosts' lives and values."[3]

When you encounter another culture, whether it's a nearby neighborhood or a far-away city, immerse yourself in it and learn about the culture from the inside-out. Here are a few ideas for how you can study culture up close.

People Watch

When you're in a public place, discreetly observe someone who comes from a different cultural background and observe what he or she does. Listen and watch longer than you would when watching people from a familiar culture. Look for similarities. What appears to be the same about how people interact with significant others, family members, strangers, and others? More important, what differences do you observe? What seems different about the body language, touch, pace, and behavior of the people you observe?

Attend Cultural Celebrations

Locate an ethnic organization in a community near you and attend one of its cultural celebrations. If at all possible, participate in the event rather than just observing from the sidelines. Ask someone to explain the significance of the activities, foods, and rituals. Get a group of friends to go to a Cinco de Mayo party together or attend a religious festival from a faith that is different from yours. If you're invited to a wedding of someone from a different cultural background, by all means go—mostly to support your friend or colleague, but with the added benefit of learning about how the wedding ceremony takes place in this culture. Observe the way a funeral takes place among various cultures. If at all possible, ask an insider to explain to you what's going on and the meaning associated with it.

Visit Grocery Stores

Find out where the locals shop and look at what's on the shelves. Do this in ethnic neighborhoods in your own community as well as when you travel abroad. The products sold and the way they're displayed provide some interesting cues about what's there. Or go into other stores that target niche markets like older people, outdoor enthusiasts, or tea lovers.

Eat

Food provides a powerful window into culture. Go to restaurants with ethnically different foods and explore the meanings beneath the entrees. Are the foods served authentic or are they adaptations for the local pallet (e.g., the Chinese food served in many Western locations is significantly different from the typical fare in China. And in many years of traveling to China, I've yet to see a "take-out" box with wire handles or a fortune cookie).

KNOWLEDGE

Better yet, share a meal with someone who comes from the culture of the food you're eating and see if he or she can offer some perspective about various dishes. A Thai friend might not be able to offer the history behind pad thai any more than you might know what's behind some of your own cultural favorites. But at the very least, ask if your friend ate this growing up and what memories, if any, are associated with this dish.

Look at Art

Visit an art museum when you travel or simply notice the art that is displayed in public places. What kinds of pictures, if any, are hanging up in restaurants and stores? What do you see in people's homes or in office settings? What can you learn about the culture based on the architecture and the layout of a city?

Notice whether solid, straight edges and moldings permeate interior design, architecture, and paintings. Or does the art reflect more fluid, seamless lines? Does the music follow a pattern with fixed pitches and precision, or is it more incremental and blurred?

I recently visited an art gallery in Melbourne, Australia, filled with Aboriginal art. This provided me with a whole different perspective on the indigenous people in Australia than what I've learned from books and lectures describing them. A painting, a sculpture, or a graphic novel portray norms of a culture that are hard to understand through words and language alone. We have to beware of assigning one artist's portrayal to how everyone in that culture sees things. But art provides a multidimensional perspective on a culture.

There are countless other ways to learn about culture wherever you are. Roam the local streets, take in local events, and talk to taxi drivers. I love talking to taxi drivers wherever I go. They usually have strong opinions about almost everything. They're watching and listening to various people all day long and hear things that aren't meant for public consumption. Or talk with elderly people. Ask them how this place has changed during their lifetime.

Find ways to experience something more than the faux culture that exists in most places where you travel and instead, look for the authentic life of a place. For example, you can be at the Grand Palace in downtown Bangkok surrounded by thousands of camera-carrying tourists who linger at Starbucks and KFC. Or you can hop on a city bus and be instantly engulfed by locals without a tourist in sight. The real experiences are there to be had. You just have to seek them out. Free yourself from thinking you have to catch all the "must-see" attractions and go for the more authentic, local experiences. This is a fun and powerful way to increase your CQ Knowledge.

KNOWLEDGE

2. GOOGLE SMARTER

If you need information on anything—movie times, the temperature in Capetown, or how to deal with sinus pressure—the first default for many of us is Google, the source of all knowledge. Search engines and the Internet provide us with unprecedented amounts of information. And the vast resources on the Web can be powerful for enhancing CQ Knowledge. But how do we begin to wade through the endless information to gather input that's truly helpful? How do we figure out whether the blog posted by someone about what's going on in China is accurate?

Edna Reid, an expert in intelligence gathering, consults with leaders around the world to help them gather information that will truly enhance their CQ Knowledge. Reid teaches how to maximize the powers of Google. Let's assume that you're going to Qatar and you want to get more than just a Wikipedia or travel site description about the country. Here are a few ways to refine your search:

- To search specific kinds of sites related to Qatar, search using specific domain extensions (e.g., .org, .edu, .gov). Here are some examples:
  - To search government sites with information about Qatar, enter: "Qatar site.gov."
  - To search educational sites (universities, etc.) with information about Qatar, enter: "Qatar site.edu."
  - To search Qatar-based sites about Qatar, search: "Qatar site.qa."
- Remember that quotes limit the search to finding the exact combination of words you enter (e.g., "Qatar commerce" will find only information where those two words occur together).

- Next, wield the power of "Advanced Search" in Google. Here you designate much more specifically what you do and don't want to have come up in your search results. The "Advanced Search" link is usually just to the right of the main search window on Google's home page. A few examples of how you can do an advanced search:

  - You can limit your search to only retrieving pdf documents by using the "File type" menu.

  - You can search specific websites. For example, you can limit your search to anything written about Qatar on an IBM website.

  - You can limit the date range in order to pull up only the most recent information or for a specific time period.

- Go to Google Scholar (scholar.google.com) to search academic and research-based material related to your topic. You'll notice that the search results indicate the number of times the publication has been cited by others.[4]

With just a few more clicks and keystrokes, you can gain much more credible information from the Internet. When looking for country or culture-specific information, narrow your search to get more accurate and helpful information.

KNOWLEDGE

3.   INCREASE YOUR GLOBAL AWARENESS

Global awareness is a crucial part of growing CQ Knowledge. It's difficult to thoughtfully engage cross-culturally without a global perspective. Knowing that Singapore is not part of China and understanding that it's not a land of squalor is an important (and elementary) point of understanding before engaging with a Singaporean or someone else from the region. Speaking about African countries as specific nations rather than making arbitrary statements about all of Africa as if Nigeria, Sudan, and Morocco are all the same place is again pretty basic, but it's surprising how often this is a problem and the negative consequences that result.

In addition, a basic purview of major historical and current events around the world is important on so many levels. For one thing, when you know even the basic history between Japan and China, it makes you think differently about what might be going on when a Japanese and Chinese colleague are interacting. For years, Japan attempted to dominate China politically and militarily to secure its vast resources. It's unlikely that a Japanese and Chinese colleague are consciously thinking about the historical dynamics between their nations every time they interact, but it might be implicitly shaping what occurs based on the "history" lessons they received growing up. And if you're traveling to the country hosting the World Cup or during a major election there but never mention it, it will probably suggest an ethnocentric ignorance. You might think, *I'm not being ethnocentric. I'm just not into sports or politics,* but that's not the point. Referencing these culturally significant events demonstrates some awareness and interest in what's going on in the local setting.

It requires some intentional effort to increase your global consciousness because many news outlets only report on fads, trends, or events for a local market. And many families and educational systems spend little time teaching much value for understanding what's going on around the world. But once again, an informed use of the Internet can pretty quickly offer some decent insights.

Americans, in particular, are notorious for our abysmal global consciousness. One of the things that fuels disdain for the United States is the sense that many American know little about the world beyond themselves.

Here are a few ways to enhance your global consciousness:

- Visit BBC news (http://news.bbc.co.uk/) for one of the more robust purviews of world events. The "In Pictures" link is one of my favorite ways to get a quick global purview of the day around the world.

- Read *The Economist* for a survey of current events internationally.

- Check out http://www.worldpress.org for a quick overview of current stories globally.

- Visit http://www.languagemonitor.com/ to see the top ten words of the year.

- Tune in to public broadcasting.

- Learn to ask good questions when you're with people from different parts around the world. Most love to talk about their culture and share some of the timely news stories in the region.

There's little excuse for global ignorance in today's technologically connected world. There's no need to be a walking newscast, but even two or three minutes a day spent scanning major global events goes along way in raising your CQ Knowledge.[5]

4. GO TO THE MOVIES OR READ A NOVEL

Literature and film provide a visceral way to see the world through someone else's eyes. It's one thing to understand the concepts and principles of culture described in nonfiction books like this one. But there's another kind of insight and perspective provided by seeing how cultural dynamics impact the characters and subject matter of a good movie, novel, or memoir.

Almost any novel, memoir, or movie is filled with cultural dynamics because culture is everywhere. Notice how culture shapes what occurs. And look for storylines that specifically take place in a different culture. How does culture influence the way characters interact with their coworkers, friends, and family? How does conflict get resolved? Even if the story presents an inaccurate stereotype, you'll encounter individuals who defy stereotypes in real life, too.

Stories provide a much more dynamic experience with culture than most principle-based business and professional books. And they're much more true to how we experience culture—in the context of life, relationships, and a myriad of other circumstances. As you follow a story, think about how you would manage the various individuals. What if the lead character was your boss? How would you relate to her as a peer? To which characters are you most drawn? Which ones rub you the wrong way? How might culture explain some of these reactions?

As compared to when you're actually interacting with someone from a different culture, books and movies allow you to be an observer rather than having to fully participate and worry about your effectiveness and potentially offensive behavior. You can sit back and observe what's occurring. This gives you the mental reserves to study the influence culture has on what's going on and to learn.

National Geographic contributor Daisann McLane suggests a twist on this idea by encouraging us to go to cinemas when we travel abroad to see the destination with new eyes. She writes, "I've had some of my most interesting experiences watching films 'out of context.' Like the times I was the only American in a youth club in Croatia showing Spike Lee's *Do the Right Thing* and ended up explaining the slang."[6] And, of course, watching a Bollywood epic when you're visiting Mumbai can provide a whole different level of insight into Indian culture—both the film itself and the experience of going to the movie. Go to a movie, read a good story, and enhance your CQ Knowledge in the process.

KNOWLEDGE

5. LEARN ABOUT CULTURAL VALUES

One of the most important strategies for growing CQ Knowledge is understanding a core set of cultural values. Cultural values are a society's ideas about what is good, right, fair, and just. Researchers have developed a variety of ways to categorize these values in order to quickly compare one culture with another. We shouldn't carelessly stereotype an entire culture with these values because there will be individuals and subcultures within a larger culture that are exceptions to these norms. But these values provide a helpful starting point for understanding cross-cultural relationships and situations. They give you an educated guess about how someone from a culture is likely to approach something.

The influence of these values is usually subconscious to most people within a culture—including ourselves. However, cultural values play a powerful role in shaping the thoughts and behaviors of individuals, organizations, and societies, regardless of whether they realize it. It's neither better nor worse for an individual or culture to be one way or another along these values. But they do play a powerful role in how we live and work.

I've written more extensively about these cultural values in other books along with offering a deeper discussion about the leadership implications of each of them.[7] But here's a quick overview of some of the most important cultural values you should understand.

Individualism—Collectivism
The extent to which personal identity is defined in terms of individual or group characteristics.

Highly individualist cultures, such as the United States or Australia, emphasize the rights and responsibilities of the individual. Collectivist cultures like China and Jordan prioritize the rights and needs of groups.

Individualism	Collectivism
Australia	China
United States	Jordan
Individualism: Individual goals and rights are more important than personal relationships.	*Collectivism:* Personal relationships and the benefit of the group are more important than individual goals.

Power Distance
The extent to which differences in power and status are expected and accepted.

Low power-distance cultures such as Israel and Canada diminish the significance of formal titles and roles and prefer flat organizational charts. High power-distance cultures such as India and Brazil think titles and clear authority lines are important indicators of how to relate and behave.

Low Power Distance	High Power Distance
Canada	Brazil
Israel	India

KNOWLEDGE

Low PD: Status difference is of little importance; empowered decision making is expected across all levels.	*High PD:* Status difference should shape social interaction; authority should make decisions.

Uncertainty Avoidance
The extent to which risk is reduced or avoided through planning and guidelines.

Low uncertainty avoidance cultures such as Hong Kong and the United Kingdom have a higher tolerance and comfort with ambiguity and risk. High uncertainty avoidance cultures such as Russia and Japan look for ways to prevent uncertainty and risk.

Low Uncertainty Avoidance	High Uncertainty Avoidance
Hong Kong	Japan
United Kingdom	Russia
Low UA: Focus on flexibility and adaptability; tolerate unstructured and unpredictable situations.	*High UA:* Focus on planning and reliability; uncomfortable with unstructured or or unpredictable situations.

Cooperativeness—Competitiveness*
The extent to which achievement and competition are valued in contrast with a priority on social relationships and emotions.

Cultures that have a cooperative orientation such as Chile and the Netherlands value a more collaborative, nurturing approach to situations. Cultures with a more competitive orientation like Hungary and Japan have a more aggressive and assertive approach to life.

Cooperative	Competitive
Chile	Hungary
Netherlands	Japan
Cooperative: Emphasis on cooperation and nuturing behavior. A high value placed on relationships and family.	*Competitive:* Emphasis on assertive behavior and competition. A high value placed on work, task accomplishment, and achievement.

*This value is sometimes referred to as femininity and masculinity, but I've moved away from those labels in my work rather than perpetuate socially constructed, gender stereotypes. But the idea of low versus high competitiveness is important, regardless of how it is labeled.

Time Orientation
The extent to which there's a willingness to await success.

Short-term cultures such as Australia and the United States emphasize instant results. Long-term cultures such as South Korea and Brazil are more interested in long-term innovation and success, even if it means delayed gratification.

Short-Term	Long-Term
Australia	Brazil
United States	South Korea
Short Term: See future as unpredictable and value immediate outcomes more than long-term benefits.	Long Term: Value long-term planning, willing to sacrifice short-term outcomes for long-term benefits.

KNOWLEDGE

Context

The extent to which communication is direct and emphasizes roles and implicit understanding.

Low-context cultures such as Israel and Canada will usually post a lot of signs and directions and emphasize very direct, thorough communication. High-context cultures such as Saudi Arabia and Mexico presume individuals know how to get along more intuitively where explicit communication is unnecessary.

Low Context	High Context
Canada	Mexico
Israel	Saudi Arabia
Low Context: Emphasize explicit words; value direct communication.	*High Context:* Emphasize harmonic relationship and implicit understanding; value indirect communication.

Doing—Being

The extent to which action and results are emphasized and valued.

Doing cultures such as the United States and Austria are extremely task-focused and outcome oriented. In contrast, being cultures such as Sweden and Brazil prioritize relationships and social networks and live for the moment.

Doing	Being
Austria	Sweden
United States	Brazil

KNOWLEDGE

Doing: Task completion takes precedence over social commitments; there is clear separation of the two.	*Being:* Social commitments and task completion are equally important; there are diffuse boundaries between the two.

KNOWLEDGE

These dimensions of cultural values are most often used to describe national cultures (e.g., the individualism of the United States versus the collectivism of Yemen). But the values may also apply to subcultures. For example, one business setting will use a very team-based approach to leadership and decision making (low power distance) and another will use a strong top-down structure (high power distance). The same is true among various generations, which often gravitate toward one direction or the other along these value sets.

Robert doesn't have time to learn everything about Yemeni culture and even if he did, it might be largely irrelevant to Sana, given that she's never lived there. But a broad understanding of the values often held by Arab Americans would help him ask much better questions in the interview and enhance his understanding of Sana's responses. And if Sana uses cultural values to understand the subcultures of Indianapolis, the telecom company, and Robert's background, it will at least give her a starting point for making sense of what she encounters.

Many resources (e.g., online, books, classes) provide a thorough explanation of cultural values with designations of where various nations lie along these continua.[8] It's increasingly difficult to characterize entire national cultures as being oriented one way vs. another, so we have to apply these values cautiously. But understanding the dimensions themselves is a vital tool for understanding some important ways that cultures differ. Just don't overextend their use by assigning a cultural value to every situation and person in a particular culture. One of the most helpful ways to use these cultural values is to understand your own personal orientation in each of these areas. To learn more about taking an *Individual Cultural Values Inventory*, visit www.CulturalQ.com.

KNOWLEDGE

6. EXPLORE YOUR CULTURAL IDENTITY

None of us are merely objective observers of culture. We're all products of culture, and we all play a part in advancing and morphing the cultures of which we're part. As a result, another important strategy for growing your CQ Knowledge is to understand your own cultural identity. This is often the hardest culture to understand and see because it's so ingrained in us, and it's largely subconscious. We've grown up with a certain set of implicit rules and assumptions by which to live life and view the world and without CQ Knowledge, it's easy to assume, that's just the way the world is.

National cultures usually play the strongest influence in how we see the world. But other cultures where we're immersed also play a profound role in how we think and behave.

Identify the cultures that most powerfully influence you. Address the following:

- What national and ethnic cultures have most significantly shaped you?

- What other subcultures have most powerfully shaped how you think and behave (consider subcultures like universities, the profession you're in, your major at school, a corporate culture, religious affiliations, sexual identity, generational dynamics, physical disability groups, etc.)?

- Zero in on the one or two cultural contexts that most strongly define who you are today.

After you identify the cultures that have most powerfully shaped you, begin to think about questions like these in relationship to one or more of these cultures:

- What does "success" look like in this culture? How about failure?

KNOWLEDGE

- What professions have the highest salaries? Societies tend to pay the most money for what's most valued (e.g., entertainers, government officials, cosmetic surgeons, etc.).

- What's the role of family?

- How are decisions made?

- Who holds the most power?

- Who's given more respect—the old or the young?

- Where does your country of origin fall along the cultural values listed in the previous strategy? How about other cultures that have been a significant part of your socialization?

Become a student of the history, rules, and norms of your culture. There's little hope we'll understand other cultures if we don't first understand our own. This kind of understanding provides a basis for understanding and respecting the heritage and background of other people. Where do they fall along the cultural values continua?

Ethnocentrism—believing your own culture is the right and best way to go about life—is a major roadblock to CQ Knowledge. However, bashing and deprecating everything about your culture can be equally destructive. I've fallen into that trap. There are times I've loathed being a white male, a Christian, an academic, an American, and so much more. There are aspects to all those subcultures that are worthy of embarrassment. But there are virtuous elements within each of those subcultures, too. Sometimes, when we're first exposed to different cultures and see our own culture through that new view, the tendency is to focus on all the negatives of our own culture. A commitment to understanding our own cultural background helps avoid either of these extremes and puts more emphasis on seeking to understand rather than evaluating the culture as good or bad.

Sana's trip to the Middle East was as much about helping her learn about her own cultural identity as it was about understanding the Yemeni and Jordanian cultures. And Robert's own background as a minority and a person of color could offer him significant insight into what's behind some of Sana's behavior and questions.

Your cultural background is a significant part of who you are, but there are some aspects of your identity that are unique from other individuals who share your cultural background. Examine how you're like and unlike your culture. Identify the cultural values (from the last strategy) where you're least aligned with your own culture. Do the same for other cultures with which you regularly come into contact. These are important insights because they'll likely be the places where you experience the greatest degree of conflict and tension.

Intercultural researcher Edward Hall writes, "Culture hides much more than it reveals, and, strangely, it hides itself most effectively from its own participants. *The real job is not to understand foreign cultures, but to understand one's own*"[9] (italics added). Taking the time to explore your own cultural identity will enhance your overall CQ Knowledge.

KNOWLEDGE

7. STUDY A NEW LANGUAGE

KNOWLEDGE

Languages are so much more than words. There's a clear connection between the ability to speak another language and your CQ Knowledge. Some say language is culture. The two are so seamlessly wrapped together that it's difficult to have one without the other. Language allows you to interact with people and to pick up on all kinds of things you otherwise miss. The reverse is also true. Foreign language instructors teach students about the related culture because of the integral connection between the two. Environmental factors and societal norms shape the development of language and language further shapes culture. There's a reason why there are so many different words for fish in the Norwegian language or for snow in Eskimo languages. *Wei ji* is the Chinese word for "crisis." *Wei* means danger and *ji* means opportunity. This says so much about the dominant Chinese culture, a society that has always looked to leverage hardship into opportunity. Language yanks the blinds off the window of culture and allows us to take a much better look inside.[10]

Effective study of a new language should also include learning some of the most familiar nonverbal signals and behaviors used in a particular culture. The silent language of gestures and facial expressions is a critical part of growing your CQ Knowledge.

When interacting with someone who speaks a different language, there's no substitute for learning some of the language itself. Not only does it inspire respect and gratitude, but it will help you understand how that person sees the world. We won't be able to learn the languages of most of the cultures we encounter, but studying any new language can enhance your overall CQ Knowledge. In Chapter 6, I've included another language strategy where using a few key words or phrases in another language will help you behave much more successfully in places that speak that language.

8. SEEK DIVERSE PERSPECTIVES

Most adults pursue relationships and influences that support and reinforce their own perspectives and viewpoints. One of the most valuable ways to enhance CQ Knowledge is by intentionally seeking out diverse viewpoints. The goal isn't just to minimize the differences to find out what you have in common. It's to particularly look at and learn from the differences themselves.

This strategy is most helpful when you purposely find a cultural group that represents a set of beliefs or norms that are in conflict with your own. Attend one of their gatherings or events. Go to a religious service, a rave club, or a political gathering that is least aligned with your own preferences and seek to understand what's behind the beliefs and behaviors of this group. Beware of hasty assumptions and suspend judgment for a while. Have coffee with someone who sees the world differently from you. Don't go into it trying to persuade them to see it your way. Learn from your differences. Tune in to a news source that has a bias contrary to your own opinion. Pay attention to how it affects you. When I listen to volatile rhetoric about political issues that are contrary to my own, I feel my blood pressure go up. But the challenge here is to regulate that emotion so you can learn from a different perspective than the one you have.

You don't have to abandon your beliefs and convictions. But for now, purposely put yourself into an uncomfortable setting. Convene a book club with people from varied cultural contexts. Think about how the varied cultural perspectives shape the ways individuals respond to the book. Or when given the choice to do a group project at work or for a class you're taking, seek out someone from a different background to be your partner. Even if you're from a similar ethnic background, find someone more conservative or liberal than you. If you're an atheist, find someone deeply religious or vise versa. Commit to truly entering into dialogue together and learning from each other.

KNOWLEDGE

Another way to learn from diverse viewpoints is by finding a different news source than the one you typically choose. Whether driven from a contrasting ideology or originating from a different national culture, examine how the same event gets reported differently. Read the same story on Al Jazeera, NewsAsia, and BBC. And when you travel, look for ways to read a local newspaper. If you're addicted to the *Financial Times*, *South China Post*, or *USA Today*, at least read it alongside a local paper and compare what gets reported in one as compared to the other. Skim all of it—advertisements, classifieds, public notices, and obituaries. You can gain a fascinating insight into a place by reading what does and doesn't get reported in the local news.

The same strategy can be applied at home. In the words of President Obama to his fellow Americans, "If you're someone who only reads the editorial page of the *New York Times*, try glancing at the page of the *Wall Street Journal* once in awhile. If you're a fan of Glenn Beck or Rush Limbaugh, try reading a few columns on the *Huffington Post* website. It may make your blood boil; your mind may not often be changed. *But the practice of listening to opposing views is essential for effective citizenship*"[11] (italics added).

9.   RECRUIT A CQ COACH

A CQ coach, sometimes referred to as a cultural broker or guide, can be another integral part of helping us become more culturally intelligent. This is a strategy that will help in every area of CQ. But it fits best with enhancing our CQ Knowledge. When I first started working in the university setting, my friend Andrew already had several years under his belt as a faculty member. Even though he worked for a different institution, he helped me understand things like tenure, academic freedom, faculty governance, and much more. Friends like Naville, Soon, Soo Yeong, and Judy have spent years helping me understand Southeast Asia. My list of CQ coaches continues in places and cultures around the world.

A CQ coach can be a valuable asset in any cultural context. The challenge is finding one who can truly play that role. For example, sometimes outsiders, like an expat, can be a valuable guide because they too are bridging from another culture into this one. But I've also encountered expats who have very skewed, ill-informed understandings of the cultures where they live. Locals can be good coaches, but we also have to beware of assuming that the people who live in a culture make the best guides. They often lack the objectivity needed, too.

An effective CQ coach will use questions to guide us and offer support and feedback. It should be an individual who is careful not to oversimplify things while also offering some helpful, neutral stereotypes. Whoever it is, we have to remember the importance of not generalizing based on the advice we receive from any one individual. Intercultural expert Craig Storti says,

> What [individuals] say may be true for people of their own age group, level of education, socioeconomic background (not to mention caste, religion, region or locality, sex, and experience) but not for other sectors of society. Ask a Montana rancher and a Manhattan banker what proper behavior or dress is at a dinner party and try to generalize from their answers![12]

KNOWLEDGE

Select CQ coaches carefully. Some things to look for include:

❏ Can they distinguish what's different about this culture from others?

❏ Do they demonstrate self-awareness? Other-awareness?

❏ Are they familiar with your culture, including your national culture and your vocational culture (e.g., engineering or health care)?

❏ Have they worked across numerous cultures themselves?

❏ Do they ask lots of questions to help you discover the culture, or simply "tell" you?

❏ Can they articulate what kinds of personalities often get most frustrated in this culture?

A CQ coach with a good measure of multicultural awareness will serve you well. Reading an explanation about cultural issues in a book or going through a cross-cultural exercise is very different from receiving an explanation from someone who has lived through what we're experiencing. Research indicates that expatriates and travelers who have cultural mentors fare better than those without them.[13] One of the greatest things CQ coaches do is to help you know what kinds of questions you should ask of yourself and others as you move into this assignment.

BACK AT THE OFFICE

Sana would be better prepared for her interview with Robert and other managers in Indianapolis with a stronger understanding of the mainstream Midwest culture. Even though she's lived in Michigan all her life, she's been relatively insulated within the Arab American community surrounding greater Detroit. She should be careful not to stereotype Robert, but with some grasp of cultural values, she could at least think about whether Robert wearing a suit is a reflection of his African American values for dress and appearance.

If I were Sana, I'd be pretty taken aback by the confrontation with her aunts in Yemen. To feel defensive in that kind of situation is normal. But if Sana can see beyond the confrontation and think about how her lifestyle and upcoming move may appear through her aunts' cultural lens, it might help her deal with the anger of being called an infidel. One of the things about CQ, though, is that it's a two-way street. So Sana's aunts would also be helped by some cultural understanding of life for Sana and Haani back in the United States. Before immediately making accusations, a greater degree of CQ Knowledge would, at the very least, allow them to approach the potentially offensive conversation differently.

As for Robert, even though he's a minority, he seems ignorant that many other ethnic minorities have been born and raised in the United States, too. It's bizarre, though commonplace, that he assumes Sana wasn't born in the States. And if Robert knew more about the cultural values of individualism vs. collectivism, he might be less thrown off by Sana's request to have Haani meet him. It would be a very reasonable request from a collectivist perspective for a spouse—and in particular, the husband in many Middle Eastern cultures—to want to know if he can trust his partner's boss. Robert comes from a more collectivist culture himself, compared to the mainstream, dominant culture in the Midwest.

But because of his marriage to Ingrid and having lived and worked largely in the dominant, professional culture for twenty years, he's likely to be as much a product of that individualist subculture as of his more collectivist upbringing on the south side of Chicago.

And what about Robert's friend Sharon advising him about the different rules for business in the Middle East—where her colleague Alvin was expected to pay a tip (bribe?) to get his paperwork processed? Sharon is right about one thing—business in different parts of the world operates by a different set of rules. We have to be careful to presume that different rules and practices are bad simply because they're different or unfamiliar. But there's good reason to be concerned about the many ethical dilemmas involved in a situation like the one that faced Alvin. Who is most responsible for Alvin's dilemma—the immigration officer, the country that doesn't pay the officer adequately, or other developed nations and their companies that don't address this issue or who actually perpetuate the practice? Increased CQ Knowledge will caution Robert from stereotyping all Middle Eastern companies as operating this way. But it will also alert him to the idea that written policies, procedures, and contracts don't have the same binding power in high-context societies as do commitments made through relationships and time spent together.

INCREASING YOUR CQ KNOWLEDGE

An abundance of information is available about various cultures. Don't be overwhelmed. Start with a couple of these strategies to improve your CQ Knowledge. Then try another one.

Identify two strategies you can begin using to enhance your CQ Knowledge.

KNOWLEDGE

	Strategy	Category
❑ 1.	Study culture up close.	Business/Cultural Systems
❑ 2.	Google smarter.	
❑ 3.	Improve your global awareness.	
❑ 4.	Go to the movies or read a novel.	Interpersonal/Cultural Values
❑ 5.	Learn about cultural values.	
❑ 6.	Explore your cultural identity.	
❑ 7	Study a new language.	Socio-Linguistics
❑ 8.	Seek diverse perspectives.	Leadership
❑ 9.	Recruit a CQ coach.	

Which one will you try first? When?

CHAPTER **5**

CQ STRATEGY

It's one thing to be motivated to engage in cross-cultural work and relationships and to have some basic understanding about how cultures are alike and different. But the real lynchpin between CQ Drive and Knowledge with how we actually behave cross-culturally is CQ Strategy. CQ Strategy asks the question: *Am I aware, and can I plan appropriately in light of the personal and cultural dynamics involved?* This is one of the most important benefits of the CQ difference—the ability to apply your motivation and understanding to real-life situations.

CQ Strategy: The extent to which you are aware of what's going on in a cross-cultural situation and your ability to use that awareness to manage those situations effectively.

Key Question: What do I need to plan in order to be effective in this cross-cultural situation?

As Sana leaves the interview, she calls Haani. "That was a waste of time! I'll never get the job." She tells him everything that happened, including the fact that Robert started the interview thirty minutes late and was the only person in the office dressed in a suit and tie. As she replays it to Haani, she's convinced Robert was making a power play right from the start. "Why else would he wear a dark suit and start the interview so late?" she asks. "He wanted to make it clear who the boss is! As if I don't know!"

"That's crazy!" Haani responds. "He's the CFO, so that's why he's wearing a suit. And African Americans are always late, just like your parents. It's a cultural thing."

She knows her head covering is probably uncomfortable for potential employers. She wonders if she should have gone to the interview without it. Many of her Muslim friends back in Detroit haven't worn one since high school. They see it as very old-school. But Sana doesn't feel like her hijab is a symbol of oppression. She actually feels more comfortable wearing it. And it's better that an employer sees her with it now than surprising the company after she's hired.

Meanwhile, Robert has the big meeting about the Middle Eastern acquisition in a couple of hours and there's no time to prepare. From reviewing all the reports they've received, it seems like working toward a win–win deal with this Middle Eastern company is a no-brainer. But Robert can't shake his fears from Sharon's story about the Singaporean who had to bribe his way into doing work in the Mideast. Robert and his company pride themselves on their integrity and transparency. In fact, the U.S. Department of Justice just asked Robert to come represent the company at an antitrust summit they're doing in D.C. because of the company's exemplary practices.

Robert decides, *You know what? I'm a bottom-line kind of guy, so they might as well know that about me now. I'm just going to tell them what Sharon told me and see how they respond. Their response alone will tell us volumes. If we're disclosing all our financials, the least they can do is respond to a concern about corrupt business practices.*

A week later, Robert has interviewed all the job candidates, and it's clear Sana is the most qualified person for the job. Her references gave her rave reviews. She scored well on the assessments administered by the human resources office. And she demonstrates the needed balance between administrative capabilities and people skills.

Robert is known for being a guy who makes decisions quickly. But this one is unusually hard for him. He calls her voice mail, hoping she won't pick up. She doesn't. He just wants to see if he can detect any foreign accent when she speaks. Nope. There's nothing about her voice on the recording that would indicate she isn't a native Midwesterner. It's not that Robert has anything against foreigners. After all, he married one. It's his clients he's worried about. They aren't as accepting as he is. He should know. He puts up with their racist comments and behavior all the time. His natural voice is loud and exuberant, but he's learned to speak more quietly lest people be fearful of a boisterous, 6'2" African American man in corporate finance. So what will his clients do if they show up at his office and see someone like Sana? Most of the people he deals with aren't going to know how to respond to someone who looks like her.

Robert catches himself. *What am I thinking? It seems like every week someone talks about how "articulate" and "eloquent" I am.* He doesn't speak any differently than Joe, the CIO in the office next door, but Joe's white so no one thinks to point out that he's articulate. Is Robert doing the very thing to Sana that has been done to him all his life by the good old boys?

Robert refuses to discriminate. This is a moment of truth. He decides to hire Sana. He's going to ignore her ethnic and religious background and just treat her as a human being. He thinks, *No matter what we look like, we're all the same.*

WHAT'S CQ STRATEGY GOT TO DO WITH IT?

CQ Strategy is your level of awareness and your ability to plan in light of your cultural understanding. This dimension of cultural intelligence is what initially intrigued me most. I found a lot of material that dealt with learning about different cultures and some helpful hints about how to behave. But through my own experience and research, I knew that someone could be an expert on all things cross-cultural and still fail miserably. There's a whole set of subtle, behind-the-scenes issues that have to be understood. It's one thing to know that you and your culture approach risk differently than another culture (uncertainty avoidance); but can you actually use that understanding to behave in ways that are useful and respectful? CQ Strategy is the lynchpin between understanding and action. This is what really launches you into a different league of players out on the multicultural field.

Both Sana and Robert would be helped significantly by increased CQ Strategy. Some of the indicators of Sana's CQ Strategy lie in her assumptions about Robert being dressed in a suit and his tardiness to the interview. Robert's identification with being a minority is an important thing to pay attention to as is his decision to ignore the differences between Sana and him and to be direct with his Middle Eastern guests about his fear regarding corruption. These demonstrate low CQ Strategy.

Again, CQ Strategy asks the question: *Can I anticipate and plan appropriately in light of the personal and cultural dynamics involved?* CQ Strategy is a weak capability among many individuals tested because many of us are forced to function at a frenetic pace with little space for deeper thought and reflection. CQ Strategy is unlikely to be developed apart from intentional, focused thought. The technical term for CQ Strategy is *meta-cognition*, which means "thinking about thinking." This is what happens when you transcend your immediate emotions and thoughts and try to observe them from outside yourself. And it's what happens when you do that with others. Many refer to this as reflection-in-action, or reflective practice.

You demonstrate high CQ Strategy when you draw on your cultural understanding to develop a plan for a cross-cultural situation or assignment. With high CQ Strategy, you're better able to monitor, analyze, and adjust your behavior in different cultural settings. You're conscious of what you need to know about an unfamiliar culture, but you hold your assumptions about that culture loosely until you actually experience it. Individuals with high CQ Strategy often have developed this capability intuitively or have personalities (e.g., introverts) that are more naturally inclined toward analysis and reflection.

ASSESSING YOUR CQ STRATEGY

How is your CQ Strategy? To what extent can you make sense of culturally diverse experiences and plan in light of shifting realities? Based on the feedback report that accompanies the online *CQ Self-Assessment*, what overall CQ Strategy score did you receive?

Overall CQ Strategy:_____
   Did you rate yourself low, medium, or high compared
   to others who have completed the *CQ Self-Assessment*?
   (circle one)

   Low   *Medium*   *High*

From what you're learning about CQ Strategy in this chapter, are you surprised by the results? Keep in mind that the self-assessment is just one snapshot of your view of your CQ capabilities at a particular point in time. But it's worth considering the results given the high level of reliability found in the assessment as used among individuals around the world.

In order to dig more deeply into your CQ Strategy, the assessment also helps you assess your cultural understanding in three specific areas of CQ Strategy (awareness, planning, and checking). There has been extensive research examining the way these various dimensions of meta-cognition influence your overall awareness and planning for multicultural situations.[1] Write your scores for each of the following and note the descriptions of these sub-dimensions:

Awareness: _____

This is the extent to which you're aware of the personal and cultural dynamics occurring in a multicultural situation. A high score means you're very alert to and observant of what's occurring within yourself and others during cross-cultural interactions. A low score means you rated yourself low on your level of awareness during cross-cultural experiences.

Planning: _____

This is the extent to which you take the time to anticipate how to best engage in a cross-cultural situation. A high score means you plan ahead and think intentionally about how you should relate and work in a multicultural situation. A low score means you place limited value on planning ahead for cross-cultural scenarios.

Checking: _____

This is the extent to which you monitor whether you are behaving appropriately in a cross-cultural situation. A high score means you are continually checking to see if your plans were appropriate. A low score means you don't spend much time testing the accuracy of your assumptions and plans for a multicultural situation.

These three sub-dimensions of CQ Strategy—awareness, planning, and checking—are the scientific bases for the strategies that follow. You'll see these sub-dimensions alongside the list of strategies at the beginning of the next section. Not every strategy fits perfectly with a single sub-dimension, but the strategies have been organized according to the sub-dimension with which they are most closely associated. Use your scores from the sub-dimensions of CQ Strategy to help you pinpoint which strategies to use first (presumably, the strategies that go with the sub-dimension where you scored lowest).

IMPROVING YOUR CQ STRATEGY

The following section is a list of strategies to help you improve your CQ Strategy. All these strategies are rooted in science and research on meta-cognition and the ability to engage in flexible thinking for multicultural situations. They stem from the three sub-dimensions of CQ Strategy (awareness, planning, and checking). The point is not for you to use all these strategies right now. There are many paths to increasing CQ Strategy. Start with a couple that interest you.

1. Notice; don't respond. 2. Think widely. 3. Focus deeply. 4. Journal.	Awareness
5. Plan social interactions. 6. Manage expectations. 7. Create checklists.	Planning
8. Reframe a situation. 9. Test for accuracy. 10. Ask better questions.	Checking

STRATEGY

1. NOTICE; DON'T RESPOND

One way to improve your CQ Strategy is to intentionally put up your antenna to take note of what's going on in a multicultural situation. The key to using this strategy successfully is to notice without responding to what you see. Don't rush to make sense out of what you observe. This is counterintuitive because our natural impulse is to notice something and then immediately interpret its meaning and react. We inevitably form hypotheses (actually, more often conclusions) about why people are dressed the way they are or why you only see men together at the market. But be very cautious of rushing to judgment. Notice what you're thinking and feeling but don't respond to it. Try to detach yourself. It takes effort, but it's possible to train yourself to do this. In fact, forcing your brain to stop short of making a judgmental response to something you notice can actually change the circuitry in your brain in a matter of weeks.[2]

The other day, a North American friend and I were boarding a plane in Thailand. My friend said, *"Most Asians seem so polite and reserved until you see them boarding a bus or plane. Then it's an all out pushing match! They never defer to someone else to go ahead of them."*

Whenever I'm in Asia, I almost always hear a Westerner make a comment like this. And there have been plenty of times when being shoved out of the way by a sweet old Chinese woman leaves me just a little miffed myself. But in the words of anthropologist Grant McCracken, when we notice things like this, we need to stop and ask, *"Hmm, I wonder why that is?"*[3] Rather than jumping to conclusions, look at something that puzzles you and think about it for a long time.

If you spend enough time noticing the masses of people in Asia, for example, you'll begin to see that pushing is often a necessity here. Many times, you can't survive here using the schoolteacher's mantra, "Everyone will get a turn. Just wait in line." Everyone *won't* get a turn. Some are going to get left behind, and a certain level of aggressiveness becomes a means to survival.

Gregory David Roberts, in his phenomenal novel *Shantaram*, refers to this as the doctrine of necessity. He suggests that the amount of force and violence necessary to board a train in India is no less and no more than the amount of politeness and consideration necessary to ensure that the cramped journey is as pleasant as possible. Roberts writes, "If there were a billion Frenchmen or Australians or Americans living in such a small space, the fighting to board the train would be much more, and the courtesy afterward much less."[4]

Granted, the people boarding the plane with my friend and me already had a "guaranteed" seat. But we don't unlearn our survival strategies quickly, even if they don't apply at the moment.

For Sana to take note of how Robert is dressed compared to everyone else in the office is a good sign of awareness. But it's dangerous when she assumes she knows why he wore a suit today. The same applies to the thirty-minute delay in starting the interview. Both Sana and Haani are rushing to judgment about why that occurred. Robert has also made some underlying judgments, presumably based on Sana's name and her head covering. He would have no other reason to conclude she's a Muslim.

Look around you. Notice and ask, *"Hmm. I wonder why that is."* Why is the airport organized like this? What's behind the clothes people wear to work here? What does this newsletter teach you about this organization? With time, you'll be able to form some accurate interpretations about these things. For now, suspend judgment. Notice, but don't respond.

STRATEGY

2. THINK WIDELY

Another way to enhance your CQ Strategy is to train your mind to think more broadly. Your level of comfort with this is somewhat related to your personality. Every individual has what psychologists call a *category width* (see Figure 5-1). This is the extent to which you're comfortable with things that don't neatly fit into one category or another. Your category width is shaped by your personality, your upbringing, and your culture.

Figure 5-1 Category width.

Narrow Categorizers

Right	Different	Wrong

Broad Categorizers

Right	Different	Wrong

Based on concepts in T. F. Pettigrew, "The Measurement and Correlates of Category Width as a Cognitive Variable," *Journal of Personality* 26 (1958): 532–544.

I was brought up with very narrow category width. My grandfather had a mantra that was often repeated in our home: "*When in doubt, don't do it.*" The idea was to avoid anything in the "gray areas." And frankly, there were very few things in our home that were deemed *gray*. My parents had a lot of rules about the ways I could dress, the kinds of social events I could go to, how long my hair could be, and a lot more. In some ways, it made for a very stable upbringing. There wasn't much ambiguity. Most of the world could be neatly divided into right or wrong.

STRATEGY

Going away to college, doubting my faith, and traveling internationally broadened my category width significantly. I still have things that I consider to be right and wrong. In fact, there are things I put into those categories that I never thought much about as a kid—poverty, the environment, human rights, and so on. But on the whole, I have much wider category width today. So many things seem neither right nor wrong but simply different. Think about how you respond to that statement; it's probably some indication of your own category width. If you're repulsed by what feels like my loosey-goosey view, it probably indicates you have a more narrow category width. There's nothing wrong with that (see—I have wide category width, so I'm fine with yours being "different" from mine); but narrow category width definitely increases your challenges when it comes to how you interpret cultural differences.

Narrow categorizers focus on differences. They watch the behavior of people from different cultures and categorize them based on what those actions would mean in one's own cultural context. For example, a narrow categorizer has certain words in mind that *should* and *shouldn't* be used by educated people, clothes that *shouldn't* appear on men, and norms for how married couples *should* relate. When there isn't a category in which to place the behavior of an individual, narrow categorizers judge it as an exception and don't entertain it as possibly being another whole category altogether.[5] Those with narrow category width are much quicker to characterize things as right vs. wrong.

Broad categorizers demonstrate more tolerance for things that might not fit into preexisting categories. And a broad categorizer puts more discrepant things in the same category. For example, broad categorizers might be quicker to acknowledge that healthy parent-child relationships in one cultural context might look different from those in one's own culture. And broad categorizers are much more apt to put "new" behaviors observed cross-culturally into a category of "different" rather than right vs. wrong or normal vs. "weird." By the way, this isn't necessarily a "liberal vs. conservative" difference. I've met liberals who were very intolerant of more conservatively minded people because of their different ideals and beliefs. You can be a "liberal" and still be a narrow categorizer.

By training your mind to think more broadly, you can increase your CQ Strategy. One practical way to do this is to see beyond the details to the big picture. Again, your comfort with this is related to your personality. And every organization and community needs both big-picture thinkers and detail-minded ones. The goal here isn't to tell the detail-oriented people to change. But it is to say that one way to improve CQ Strategy is to rise beyond a narrow focus on details for a period of time to see the big picture.

Jason Fried and David Heinemeier Hansson, the software entrepreneurs who have made tools like Basecamp and Campfire, say that when they start designing something, they always do so using a thick Sharpie marker rather than a ball-point pen. For them, pen points are too fine and tempt them to get lost in the details. But a Sharpie forces them to keep sketching out the big picture before getting into all the important details.[6]

Something happens neurologically when the brain thinks widely and globally. It's hard for insights or creative thinking to happen when surrounded by lots of minutia. When you're stuck at an impasse in how to do something, often the best thing you can do is walk away from it for a bit, think about some other things, then come back to it.[7] This basic habit is one that correlates to the development of CQ Strategy. Multicultural work often requires adapting your thinking to deal with unpredictable situations. As you learn to think more broadly, you'll become better at understanding and interpreting the differences you encounter in different cultures.

STRATEGY

3. FOCUS DEEPLY

The next strategy is the mirror opposite of the last one. Just as broadening our minds can enhance our CQ Strategy by helping us deal with unpredictable situations, deep, focused thinking helps us to zero in on things we might otherwise miss. We need to train our minds to do both—think widely and focus deeply.

This strategy stems from what is often referred to as mindfulness training. *Mindfulness* is complete awareness of everything that happens within your body, mind, and consciousness. And it's applying the same kind of awareness to your environment. In a cross-cultural situation, mindfulness can help us move out of our automated habits of thinking and behavior. With little thought, we shoot off an e-mail, tell a joke, or become discouraged by an unresponsive audience. Our brain operates on autopilot as a way to cope with the many things that pull for our attention. But in a culturally diverse situation, even the task of writing e-mail and engaging in small talk, if done well, will require that we become more mindful.

To what extent are the following true of you?

- I drive places on "automatic pilot" and then wonder why I went there.

- I find it difficult to stay focused on what's happening in the present.

- I tend not to notice feelings of physical tension or discomfort until they really grab my attention.

- It seems I am "running on automatic," without much awareness of what I'm doing.

- I find myself listening to someone with one ear, doing something else at the same time.

These are the kinds of things measured by psychologists Kirk Brown and Richard Ryan in their Mindful Attention Awareness Scale.[8] The more these statements are true for you, the more you will be helped by training your mind to focus, which will, in turn, heighten your CQ Strategy.

Here are a few exercises to help you focus deeply:

- Choose an external sound and focus on it for thirty seconds. Don't let your mind wander. If it does, come back to focusing on that sound.

- Sit in silence for sixty seconds and notice where your mind goes. Follow its train of thought. What do you discover?

- Find some incoming data (e.g., a sound, sight, scent, sensation, etc.) and focus your attention on it. You could think about the feeling on your body right now as you sit in the chair, pay close attention to the texture of your clothes, or listen to the sound of a bird chirping. Do this for ten seconds right now . . . . You may have found it difficult to focus on that one input even for just ten seconds. Your mind wants to take in more. Perhaps you lost track of the feeling or sound because you started thinking about something else (e.g., When should I eat?). Your mind is always wanting to move toward the next thing, so mindfulness training is needed to slow it down and to spend more time taking in everything around us.[9]

- Walk down the street and be mindful of the sensations in your body as you place one foot down and then the other. Concentrate on the "simple" act of walking.

If you do these kinds of exercises often, you'll get better at noticing how the mind wanders, which, in turn, can move you into higher levels of consciousness as you relate and work cross-

STRATEGY

culturally. Formal training in mindfulness and meditation is another way to become more mindful. Many options are available, either from a religious or secular perspective. Deep, focused thinking will help you pick up on the subtle cues going on in multicultural encounters that otherwise go missed. Join a yoga class and improve your CQ Strategy at the same time.

STRATEGY

4. JOURNAL

Carry a journal with you for a couple of weeks or when you travel abroad and record your observations and insights about cross-cultural situations. Begin to explore the meanings behind what you observe. Just be sure to hold your interpretations and insights loosely until you've had a chance to test them more thoroughly.

Your journal is a place to write down the things you notice (the first strategy we covered). And it's a good place to begin hypothesizing why you think these things are the way they are. Don't rush to judgment but ask yourself questions.

As you journal, don't just chronicle the events of the day. Record your frustrations, describe how you feel when certain things occur, and write down questions that are stirring in your mind. Don't write for an audience. Your journal is a safe place to admit your biases, fears, insecurities, and rants.

In addition to chronicling your observations about others, pay attention to what's happening within yourself. Try to step out of your own skin to see yourself as objectively as possible. Imagine seeing yourself through the eyes of someone else.[10] This kind of self-awareness is important because most of the influences that shape how we behave are largely unknown to us. Many of our interpersonal behaviors and thought patterns are largely beyond our day-to-day awareness.[11]

Using a journal can help you with some of the other strategies in this section, like "noticing" and becoming more mindful. As already noted, CQ Strategy requires that you shut down some of your semiautomatic behavior and step outside yourself to see what you're observing, thinking, and feeling. For example, you might catch yourself feeling irritated, bored, or lonely in the midst of a cross-cultural encounter. Write about that in your journal. If you have no idea why you felt that way, that's okay. Just write it down, the very practice of which helps you transcend merely being

STRATEGY

defined by your irritation or loneliness and can do wonders for dissipating the level of energy you put toward it.

Use journaling to pay attention to internal distractions. When you're engaging cross-culturally, there's a powerful conversation occurring internally, and there are all kinds of neurological connections going on. Your nervous system is constantly processing, reconfiguring, and reconnecting trillions of connections in your brain each moment, something called *ambient, neural activity*. One study found that people hold thoughts for ten seconds on average before the mind wanders elsewhere.[12] Hold some of those thoughts captive by writing about them.

Write by hand in a physical journal rather than typing at a keyboard. There's a different kind of reflective thought process that occurs when we write by hand. This is partly because so many of us live in continuous word processor mode and the very tactile process of writing with pen and paper can nurture a slower, reflexive process that enhances valuable journaling. Journal writing enhances our ability to consider how to interpret the barrage of cues we encounter in cross-cultural situations.

Share your journaling insights with someone you trust. Some of the greatest value from journaling is in going back and reading the reflections later. Read your reflections a few weeks later, a year later, and several years later. I've been keeping journals since high school. Don't be overly impressed. It's therapeutic for me, and there have definitely been major lapses when I didn't journal for a while. But going back and reading the ways I described different circumstances and cross-cultural realities across the course of time has been an entertaining, enlightening, and sometimes painful but always transformative experience.

Writing allows us to understand ourselves and others in ways that few other things do. It forces us to slow down and become more aware of our surroundings and the meanings therein.

STRATEGY

Robert and Sana appear to be engaging in some valuable inward observation. Robert thinks about his own experience as an African American male and is considering how that shapes his decision about hiring Sana. Sana is thinking about whether it's appropriate for her to remove her head covering. If they took time to write about this—not for anyone else, just for themselves—it could play a powerful role in strengthening their CQ Strategy.

STRATEGY

5. PLAN SOCIAL INTERACTIONS

The more personal the interaction you have with someone from a different culture, the greater the potential challenge and conflict. Interacting with a restaurant server from a different culture can surface minor points of confusion or discomfort, but it has limited impact. Sitting in class next to someone from a different culture is a bit more challenging, and if you work on a project together, the challenge increases further. Marrying someone from a different cultural background is the most challenging cross-cultural encounter of all. For any of us, social gatherings are where we most often feel the cultural chasm between ourselves and people from different cultural backgrounds. Engineers from different cultural backgrounds might be relatively comfortable working together all day but find an after-hours drink together very awkward.

One way to make these encounters less uncomfortable while also improving your CQ Strategy is to plan ahead when you're going to spend time with someone from a different culture, especially if it's a social context. If I'm going to have coffee with someone who comes from a background similar to mine, chances are, I can wing it socially because I know the basic norms of small talk, appropriate topics, and humor. If, however, I'm having coffee with someone who comes from a different cultural background, spending even a few minutes thinking about the appropriate kinds of questions to ask, things to share, and ways to interact is a good way to enhance my CQ Strategy and simultaneously improve the way I interact with the individual. Some of the things learned through CQ Knowledge will help me know how to plan. When I actually get to the meeting, I might find out that my plans weren't appropriate. But the very thoughtfulness put into anticipating the meeting will strengthen my CQ Strategy. This is even more important if you need to confront someone or deal with a potentially awkward topic like money or if you have to conduct a performance review.[13]

If Robert interacts with Sana socially, he should anticipate the most appropriate way to do so. This can catch people like Robert off guard because he's an extrovert who finds social interaction easy. Some extroverts find cross-cultural, social interaction even more disorienting than introverts because extroverts are used to relating easily and naturally. Spending a few minutes thinking about how to best engage socially with someone from another cultural background will strengthen your capabilities in CQ Strategy and will more than likely strengthen the quality and effectiveness of the interaction itself.

STRATEGY

6. MANAGE EXPECTATIONS

Expectations—good, bad, or otherwise—are one of the most important things to manage when working on your CQ Strategy. The best way to manage expectations is to pay attention to them. Focus on your expectations for an upcoming cross-cultural experience. What do you anticipate happening? What do you hope to learn? What are your hopes and fears? What assumptions do you have about the people in this culture? Which judgments do you need to suspend? Write them down. Talk about them with others.

Unmet expectations are one of the most important experiences to avoid, if at all possible. David Rock, who has written extensively on the brain and leadership, writes, "Great leaders carefully manage expectations to avoid not meeting them."[14] This is a tricky balance because having goals and expectations can be motivating in and of itself. Think about how good it feels to check something off your to-do list. Expectations alter the way your brain makes sense of things, and meeting them reinforces the way the brain thinks about it. Rock says we should find ways to develop realistic expectations and then work to set them a little lower so you can come out ahead of them. When a positive expectation isn't met, reframe the situation to see if the alternative outcome might be better than what you expected at the outset.

If you're heading on an overseas trip, think about whether your expectations are appropriate. Is it realistic to come home with a contract if this is the first time you've met this client? Is it likely you'll become fluent in Spanish from your time in the immersion program, or might there be a lower expectation that's more appropriate, such as being invited to submit a proposal or getting through a shopping excursion without using English?

This strategy can also be used in our day-to-day cross-cultural encounters. When going to a class taught by someone from a different cultural background, what realistic expectations can you formulate that can make it beneficial? If you're meeting with a group of colleagues, what cultural differences will be present? How you anticipate that will shape what occurs. Accurately anticipating an experience plays a strong role in how we engage with it.

Robert Merton, an American sociologist, studied how U.S. Army recruits' expectations influenced their adaptation to the Army culture. The more accurately the privates anticipated the values and norms of the U.S. Army culture, the more likely they were to succeed and be promoted.[15] In a similar way, when global professionals accurately anticipate their job expectations in intercultural situations, they better adjust to the changes required.[16]

Whether it's entering a new work culture, marrying into a family with different ethnic or religious origins, or taking on a sales account in another country, spend time anticipating the cultural landscape.

STRATEGY

7. CREATE CHECKLISTS

Using something as simple as an old-fashioned checklist is another way you can improve your CQ Strategy. We live in a world of growing complexity, something often compounded in the midst of multicultural circumstances. Atul Gawande, a surgeon and Harvard Medical School professor, suggests an amazingly simple strategy for dealing with the complex issues of life: a checklist.[17] Military officers, airline pilots, chefs, and surgeons are realizing the value of a basic checklist. The very process of creating a checklist prior to a cross-cultural encounter can help you do the planning that's essential for CQ Strategy.

Dr. Gawande notes that the pressure and complexities of many professions today overwhelm even the best-trained practitioners. He suggests that checking things off a list can prevent potentially fatal mistakes and corner cutting. He examines checklists in cooking, aviation, construction, and investing, but focuses most on his own field—medicine—where checklists mandating simple measures like hand washing have dramatically reduced hospital-caused infections and other complications. This can have great relevance to cross-cultural work.

When you're working cross-culturally, taking the time to plan ahead by developing a checklist can prevent you from spinning off into what you've convinced yourself is just a necessary adaptation culturally, when in point of fact it might be detrimental to your overall success. The disorienting nature of doing something cross-culturally makes the value of checklists all the more important to behaving in ways that are consistent with your ideals. If you see the chance to strike a million-dollar deal, don't lose your sanity. Walk through a checklist created in more objective times to ensure that this is in the best interest of your business. Or this can even be as basic as helping other travelers plan for routine things: pack medicine, find filtered water, plan transportation from the airport, and so on.

Those leading others on cross-cultural travel experiences should prepare checklists for use in case of a crisis:

❑ Who do you need to call first?

❑ Where can you go for twenty-four-hour help?

❑ Where will you get the information you need?

❑ What's the phone number for your nearest embassy?

Improving your CQ Strategy can be as simple as creating a few checklists. The very exercise of making them is a tangible way to work on your cross-cultural planning.

STRATEGY

8.   REFRAME A SITUATION

Many of the circumstances you experience in a cross-cultural situation are beyond your control, but you can control your interpretation of what happens. Reframing or reappraisal means changing your evaluation of something. Our brains do this all the time. You hear a loud bang and think it's a gunshot. Perhaps you feel panicked only to find out that the bang is fireworks going off at a nearby celebration. Your brain immediately reorients itself from fear to excitement or ambivalence.

I often wonder how individuals survive the tragic loss of a spouse or child. I hope I never have to find out. Part of people's coping ability is tied to whether they can reframe their situation. The most successful recoveries occur when individuals can reframe their lives and future. Studies have revealed that six months after many individuals become paraplegics, they're just as happy as someone who won the lottery. This occurs because the brain recalibrates for a different set of circumstances.[18]

Reframing your interpretation of circumstances is part of how you train your brain to be flexible in multicultural situations. Reframing begins by labeling an emotion or reaction to something. Give it a name (e.g., "I'm ticked off that I can't get clear directions to the hotel). Label it but don't obsess over it, or you're likely to become more anxious. Just label it for a couple of seconds with a few words or a brief phrase. Then refocus your attention on another stimulus and channel your energy away from your frustration to solving your problem.

Reframing is most helpful in intercultural situations when you feel angry. If you're upset and the other party isn't, chances are, you're blaming the other person for doing something who's clueless he's at fault. Stopping to realize that this may be explained by cultural differences and assumptions can help you reappraise a situation rather than allowing your anger to mount and distract you.

Effective reappraisal requires the input of others. Peers can help us interpret circumstances. Particularly when you're in the midst of a highly emotional state, you need colleagues who can help you reframe the event. Talk it through. Write it down. Name it. Then move toward action.

Brain researchers have often said that stress isn't necessarily bad. It's how you deal with it that's key. When you learn to harness deep stress by reappraising a situation, you enhance your CQ Strategy and your overall effectiveness. Be conscious of things that may increase your anxiety and work out ways to reduce these before the arousal kicks in.[19]

STRATEGY

9. TEST FOR ACCURACY

Several of the tools for developing CQ Strategy are based on becoming aware, noticing what's going on, and developing appropriate plans in light of what you understand. But an essential tool to add is learning how to check back and see if your assumptions and plans were appropriate. Look for ways to test the accuracy of your observations, interpretations, and plans.[20]

I recently had a meeting with Bayani, a Filipino executive who was interested in having me do some cultural intelligence training for his company. Bayani leads a Filipino company that works throughout Asia and the Middle East. My only contact with him previously was a couple of e-mails. We found out that we were both going to be in Hong Kong at the same time, so we met for dinner one evening. Bayani had already given me a sense of what he wanted me to do for the company, but we hadn't talked at all about fees and contracts. Given that Filipino culture as a whole values building trust through relationships and time together, I had no intention of raising the issue of money in this first meeting.

To be honest, I wasn't entirely sure when and how to bring it up, because doing so in a follow-up e-mail didn't seem culturally appropriate, either. But my plan was to get to know each other, learn more about his company, talk about ways we could work together, and worry about the contractual elements later. No sooner did we place our order then Bayani said, "So how much will this cost us?" I thought he meant the restaurant bill and said, "Oh, this is on me." "No, no. Not that," he said. "I mean, to get you to come train for us." I quickly shifted gears from my plan to avert any discussion about finances but still didn't answer him directly. I was trying to read whether he was coming at me the way he thought I'd want to be dealt with as an American or whether this was really the way he wanted to negotiate. I told him we could get to that but that I'd love to learn more about him and his company before we talk about the financial arrangements. Bayani wouldn't go for it. He said, "But I want to know what the fees are." At this point, I could see my assumptions going into this meeting were not accurate at all, so I started to talk more directly about finances and Bayani responded well. It was still a risk. And I can't presume a future conversation with another Filipino will go that way. But I had to adapt on the fly, given that the interaction was going in a different direction than what I planned.

You can see how several of these strategies work together. Paying attention to the invisible cues, being aware of how I'm being perceived, and adjusting the plan I developed in light of my cultural understanding were all things that were necessary. Of course I didn't stop and think all that through at the moment. Perhaps I should have, but I was adapting on the fly. And I can give you as many examples of times when I didn't pick up on the cues and appropriately adjust my plan and floundered as a result.

Do the hard work of planning for these kinds of interactions, but then test your plan to see if it's working. Does what you're observing correlate with what experts have said about how people from a particular culture usually behave (this requires CQ Knowledge)? Continue your observation in other settings and of other individuals. As you seek additional input about the same kind of thing, does it confirm or negate the interpretations you were making? And best of all, find someone with whom you can discuss your interpretations. Use a cultural coach like we discussed in Chapter 4. Ideally, you want an individual who has an understanding of both your cultural background and the culture you're observing. When appropriate, you can also test for accuracy with the individual with whom you're interacting. Ask if what you perceive is accurate. It might take a more indirect question to get at this. Be creative. But look for ways to test the accuracy of what you perceive.

Practice this strategy by forming a hypothesis about a cultural situation you've been observing. Then test your hypothesis by reading up on it, talking to a variety of people from the cultures involved, and observing what occurs.

STRATEGY

10. ASK BETTER QUESTIONS

Questions are essential for enhancing CQ Strategy. Question your observations, question your assumptions, and find appropriate ways to ask questions of others. Listen carefully to the responses. And listen for what's *not* said. Then test out what you learn by asking the questions again in another situation and to another person. Asking good, probing questions is one of the most important ways to enhance your CQ Strategy.

One of the best ways to do this is to keep asking yourself "why?" Just as some kids keep asking their parents "Why, why, why?" this can be an effective way to get beyond surface observations to deeper insights about what's going on in a cross-cultural situation. When you experience something disorienting due to cultural differences, ask yourself *Why*. Try to dig deeper to explore what's behind something you observe.[21]

Here's how this might look for Robert to employ this strategy with himself. Robert thinks, *Hiring Sana could be a challenge for his clients.*

Why?

Because they're uncomfortable around people who look like her.

Why?

Because there are lots of implicit biases against Muslims and Arabs.

Why?

Because of 9/11, segregation, media portrayals of Muslims, and related concerns.

You get the idea. Some of the responses we give to the *why* questions might be inaccurate. So we have to ask this together with the last strategy—testing for accuracy. But the point behind the questioning strategy is to keep peeling away the layers of symptoms that can lead to a root cause of a situation. Observe a cross-cultural situation or challenge and ask yourself, *why, why, why?*

Practice this when you're sitting in a meeting and you hear someone making an argument. Or do it when you listen to a presentation or watch the news. Be careful about asking other people *why* because it can trigger defensiveness. It's better to begin with more indirect questions. For example, "Can you explain more about . . . ?" or "What do you think is going on here?"

Other questions can be used to help you dig deeper into developing CQ Strategy as you travel into different cultures. For example, some questions you can begin to ponder with a friend or in your journal are:

- What is the dominant sound here?

- What does it smell like?

- What are the most obvious objects I see?

- What *don't* I see here?

- How are young people viewed? Old people?

Useful and appropriate questions require a higher level of thinking. Learn how to use them to improve your CQ Strategy.

STRATEGY

BACK AT THE OFFICE

Robert and Sana both demonstrate some encouraging signs of being aware. They seem moderately conscious of their behavior, engage in reflection about their interactions, and think about the meaning behind what occurs. This suggests some strengths in their CQ Strategy capabilities.

They need to slow down their interpretations, however. Sana and Haani are quick to assume they know what Robert's suit and late start of the interview mean. Noticing these details is important. Making hasty judgments about what they mean is very dangerous. Instead, Sana could more cautiously hypothesize that the suit *might* be a statement of power, or it could be a personal or cultural preference for Robert to dress up despite it being "casual Friday." This could also be interpreted as a sign of respect to appear professional to interviewees, or simply necessary attire for a later commitment (e.g., a major meeting with international guests). For that matter, Robert may have simply forgotten it was casual Friday! Sana's quick judgment is typical of what most of us do unless we intentionally slow down our assumptions.

Robert's commitment to overlook the differences between Sana and him is commendable but may actually be problematic in the long run. Seeing Sana as a fellow human being is a great starting point. But he would be helped to see the great value her differences will bring to him as a person and to the job. What benefit is there in hiring people who view things just as we do? Sure—it might make for a bit less conflict, but it might also seriously undermine our ability to have a more robust, holistic approach to our work.

I have an Italian friend who says, "You Americans think, *Now that we're friends, we shouldn't argue.* But we Italians think, *Now that we're friends, we can have a real argument.*" Perhaps neither stereotype is fair. But the point is—many of us, regardless of nationality, are reticent to focus on differences because it seems divisive. Differences can be a real strength—they aren't something to be merely tolerated, but explored and leveraged!

INCREASING YOUR CQ STRATEGY

A lot of people have a decent measure of cultural understanding. But the individuals who can move into a higher level of consciousness and use that understanding to develop effective and respective relationships cross-culturally are much harder to find. Be among this minority by improving your CQ Strategy.

Identify two strategies you can begin using to enhance your CQ Strategy.

☐	1. Notice; don't respond.	
☐	2. Think widely.	Awareness
☐	3. Focus deeply.	
☐	4. Journal.	
☐	5. Plan social interactions.	
☐	6. Manage expectations.	Planning
☐	7. Create checklists.	
☐	8. Reframe a situation.	
☐	9. Test for accuracy.	Checking
☐	10. Ask better questions.	

Which one will you try first? When?

STRATEGY

CHAPTER **6**

CQ ACTION

Learning to be effective in cross-cultural situations requires more than learning a few dos and don'ts. But at the end of the day, our cultural intelligence is ultimately judged based on how we behave. CQ Action asks the question: *What behaviors should I adapt for this cross-cultural situation?* This is when we move beyond our motivation, understanding, and strategy to actually engaging in our multicultural work and relationships.

> **CQ Action:** This is the extent to which you can act appropriately in a culturally diverse situation. It includes your flexibility in verbal and nonverbal behaviors and your adaptability to different cultural norms.
>
> **Key Question:** What behaviors should I adapt for this cross-cultural situation?

Robert decides to hire Sana. Human resources asks him if he wants to call her himself, and he agrees. He's actually in Washington, D.C., for the antitrust summit he's attending on behalf of the company. He notices women all over the place with head coverings. He's visited D.C. many times. Are there more Islamic women here now, or does he just notice them more since he's been interacting with the Middle Eastern world so much over the past couple of weeks?

Speaking of which, Robert went with his gut and asked the Middle Eastern guests his question about bribes and corruption. They never really answered it, but they did assure him he could put his complete trust in their company. After all, the three executives who came to meet Robert and his colleagues are the sons of the company's founder. "You're dealing with a family-owned business, which means you should have none of these problems you're worried about," they said. Robert has always been a pretty good reader of people, so he feels at ease about moving forward. But when he said he would draft an agreement outlining the next steps for making a decision on the acquisition, they said, "Let's wait awhile. First, you must come over and spend time with us." Robert doesn't really have time for a trip to the Middle East, but he doesn't want to mess up this deal now. But what will a trip accomplish that couldn't be handled through e-mail and teleconferencing?

Robert has a few minutes at his hotel in D.C., so he calls Sana to offer her the job. In his affable way, he generously describes how excited he would be to have someone with her competence working for him, tells her what pay and benefits he's ready to offer her, and lists the many reasons why working for this company would be a great opportunity for her. And he awkwardly adds what he thinks will lighten up the conversation: "And the fact that you can help me in adding to the diversity mix around here is an added bonus!"

Robert talks for more than five minutes without Sana saying a word. She doesn't even make any sounds (such as "uh-huh" or "okay") to indicate she understands or agrees. This causes Robert to over-explain himself because he isn't sure she's tracking with him. Finally, he asks, "So what do you think? Can you start next week?" After a long pause, Sana says, "Thank you for your offer. Wouldn't it be nice for my husband and me to have dinner with you and your family this weekend?"

Robert says, "That would be nice. Maybe we could do that sometime, but not this weekend. Our schedule is packed. But we'll have a chance to meet each other's families at the Christmas party in a few weeks."

After another long pause, Sana asks, "Is the Christmas party required?" Robert tries to disguise his frustration with a courtesy chuckle and says, "Well I guess it isn't required. But I thought you were the one who wanted our families to meet. Anyway—what do you think about the job offer?"

Sana responds, "I'll need a little time. It would be really nice if we could discuss this over a meal. I'll have my husband, Haani, get back with you. And one more question. Can I have some time off on Fridays so I can go to the mosque? Of course, I'll make it up on other days, or could even come in on Sundays."

WHAT'S CQ ACTION GOT TO DO WITH IT?

CQ Action is *your level of adaptability when relating and working cross-culturally.* This is where the rubber meets the road. Can you behave in ways that are effective and respectful in cross-cultural situations while still remaining true to yourself? CQ Action is not mimicking whomever we're with. It's learning which actions need to be adapted and which don't. All four CQ capabilities are vitally important, but individuals will judge us most based on this one.

There have been all kinds of cultural behaviors going on between Robert and Sana. They really show up in their phone conversation, from Robert's attempts at humor and clarification to Sana's questions and requests. An understanding of CQ Action will help us analyze how well Robert's approach with the Middle Eastern guests worked and what was meant by their response.

Again, CQ Action asks the question: *What behaviors should I adapt for this cross-cultural situation?* This is primarily about social etiquette and appropriate behavior to suit a particular context. Etiquette doesn't usually become an issue until you engage in "bad" manners. Then suddenly, it stands out. CQ Action includes adapting your verbal and nonverbal behaviors and changing your speech acts—the way you approach different topics and situations.

Individuals with high CQ Action can draw on the other three capabilities of CQ to translate their enhanced motivation, understanding, and planning into action. They possess a broad repertoire of behaviors, which they can use depending on the context. They know when to adapt and when *not* to adapt. People with extremely high CQ Action flex their behavior appropriately without even giving it much thought. But even the most culturally intelligent individuals still encounter cultural situations that require new adaptations and behaviors.

ASSESSING YOUR CQ ACTION

How is your CQ Action? To what degree can you adapt your behavior while still remaining authentic? Based on the feedback report that accompanies the online *CQ Self-Assessment*, what overall CQ Action score did you receive?

Overall CQ Action:_____

    Did you rate yourself low, medium, or high compared
    to others who have completed the *CQ Self-Assessment?*
    (circle one)

    Low   *Medium*   *High*

From what you're learning about CQ Action in this chapter, are you surprised by the results? Keep in mind that the self-assessment is just one snapshot of your view of your CQ capabilities at a particular point in time. But it's worth considering the results, given the high level of reliability found in the assessment as used among individuals around the world.

In order to dig more deeply into your CQ Action, the inventory also helps you assess your cultural understanding in three specific areas of CQ Action (nonverbal, verbal, and speech acts). There has been extensive research examining the way these various forms of behavior influence your interactions and work cross-culturally.[1] Write your scores for each of the following and note the descriptions of these sub-dimensions:

Nonverbal: _____

This is the extent to which you can comfortably adapt your nonverbal behavior in cross-cultural situations (e.g., gestures and facial expressions). A high score means you're very natural at adapting to appropriate nonverbal behaviors, and a low score means it's a strain for you to flex your nonverbals.

Verbal: _____

This is the extent to which you modify your verbal behavior in cross-cultural situations (e.g., accent, tone, pronunciation, and of course language itself). A high score means you naturally change the way you talk when cross-cultural situations call for it, and a low score means you rated this as something that doesn't come naturally to you.

Speech Acts: _____

This is the way you alter your communication to effectively achieve a goal in a cross-cultural situation (e.g., the way you provide critique, how you express gratitude, etc.). A high score means you have a variety of ways you can use words to effectively accomplish a goal in various cultural situations. A low score means you don't change the overall ways you communicate, regardless of the cultural context.

These three sub-dimensions of CQ Action—nonverbal, verbal, and speech acts—are the scientific bases for the strategies that follow. You'll see these sub-dimensions alongside the list of strategies at the beginning of the next section. Not every strategy fits perfectly with a single sub-dimension, but the strategies have been organized according to the sub-dimension with which they are most closely associated. In this capability especially, there's tremendous overlap between the various strategies for CQ Action and the specific sub-dimensions with which they're associated. Use your scores from the sub-dimensions of CQ Action to help you pinpoint which strategies to use first (presumably the strategies that go with the sub-dimension where you scored lowest).

IMPROVING YOUR CQ ACTION

The following section is a list of strategies to help you improve your CQ Action. All these strategies are anchored in science and research on intercultural behavior, and they stem from the three sub-dimensions of CQ Action (nonverbal, verbal, and speech acts). The point is not for you to use all these strategies right now. There are many paths to increasing CQ Action. Start with a couple that interest you.

1. Develop a repertoire of social skills. 2. Be an actor. 3. Make taboos taboo.	Nonverbal
4. Use basic vocabulary. 5. Try new vocal sounds. 6. Slow down.	Verbal
7. Put yourself in a place of need. 8. Join a multicultural team.	Speech Arts

ACTION

1. DEVELOP A REPERTOIRE
OF SOCIAL SKILLS

I've continually said you don't need to master all the practices and taboos of every culture you encounter. You can't. But it's worth developing a repertoire of various social skills and drawing on the insights gained from CQ Knowledge and CQ Strategy to know when and where you should use these various skills.

Look for cues on the basic manners expected in a culture, many of which come down to nonverbal behaviors. How should you greet people, and how does that vary if it's someone with higher "status" than you? What if it's someone from the opposite gender? What should you do with your hands and feet, and how should you eat? Social etiquette is highly subject to cultural differences. Don't worry about doing this perfectly. But pick up on the different nonverbal behaviors used in various cultures and add some to your repertoire.

This strategy can also be used to work on adapting your verbal behavior and speech acts for various social occasions. For example, you can develop a variety of back-pocket questions for use in various cultures. In many African, Asian, and Latin American cultures, questions about one's extended family and their origins can be very valuable. Learn how to talk about your own family and background. In other contexts, inquiring about one's views of recent political events or even religious realities can be effective (and can be very *ineffective* in other contexts—e.g., many Chinese or American associates would be very uncomfortable discussing this with someone they don't know well).

One of the strategies for increasing your CQ Knowledge (Chapter 4) was increasing your global awareness. This can help here. When you're aware of a recent event that's happened in someone's country, it goes a long way to demonstrate respect and understanding. If you're visiting a place where they've just had a

ACTION

major victory in cricket or football, bring it up. You don't have to pretend you understand the game. In fact, a great way to demonstrate your interest in the other person's culture could be to ask for a tutorial on the game. What major elections have recently occurred that might influence the individuals you're encountering? What economic realities have been occurring? Some awareness and understanding of recent events and local concerns will increase your effectiveness when interacting cross-culturally in social interactions.

All of this broadens your repertoire of social skills. Eat a meal with your hands, practice using a bow to greet someone, and talk without having any expression on your face. This broadening of your nonverbal behaviors and social skills will improve your ability to adapt your behavior when a cultural situation requires it.

2. BE AN ACTOR

Try imitating the behaviors of someone else. Actors do this all the time. They follow police officers or spend time in hospitals to try to take on the attitudes, disposition, and concerns of the people they are trying to portray in their acting roles. Most acting lessons don't focus on learning lines and projecting the voice nearly as much as learning behavior. Good actors live in the world of imagination and take on the thoughts, emotions, attitudes, and circumstances of the character in a way that seems authentic. There's a great deal we can learn from the acting world for CQ Action.

Acting schools often help individuals deal with accents and dialects, too. Depending on the cultural intelligence of others with whom you interact, your competency may be unfairly judged if you consistently pronounce words differently from how they're pronounced by a particular group of people. Listen to how things are said and see if you can imitate it.

A good actor gets into the skin of the character he's portraying. In a similar way, the more you can identify with the individuals from various cultures, the better your ability to act like they do. First, imagine yourself in the shoes of someone from a different culture. Consider how you might see the world differently if you had been born in India or Switzerland. How might your relationship with your parents be different? How about your educational experience or your religious perspective? Then try imitating some of the behaviors you might use if you were from one of these places. Be very cautious here. If we aren't careful, mimicry can seem like mockery. In real-life cross-cultural encounters, the best approach isn't always to imitate all the behaviors we observe. *One of the crucial parts of having enhanced CQ Action is knowing when you should flex your behavior to mirror the behavior of others and when you shouldn't.* That understanding grows with the overall development of your cultural intelligence.

ACTION

The acting strategy here is less about what you do when you actually interact cross-culturally and more of an action plan for developing and enhancing your CQ Action "off-stage." Behind the scenes, respectfully practice the way you might negotiate a deal if you were a "typical" businessperson from Beijing as compared to Mexico City. Imitate the voice and style of someone you know.

The late sociologist Erving Goffman suggested that acting is something we all do everyday. We continually perform in front of others all day long, switching roles, costumes, and behavior, depending on the audience. Goffman argued that in our acting in everyday life, we strive to leave an impression that is as positive as possible, working to avoid any missed lines or off-key notes that can disrupt the entire performance.[2]

There will be times when learning to imitate the behaviors of another culture will enhance our ability to interact. Some people pick up cues and mimic quickly while others may need to practice much longer. One of my favorite things to do when I travel with my daughters is to hear them try to pick up the local language or dialect. It's fun to hear them repeat the sounds they hear. They do a way better job than me of imitating the true local style. When done respectfully and thoughtfully, mimicry can be a fun way to work on growing CQ Action.

It would be inauthentic for Sana and Haani to abandon all of their cultural background. But they could benefit by spending some time at home imitating how the stereotypical Midwestern couple in their stage of life would behave. This will help them identify with the people they're going to continually encounter in Indianapolis.

Many actors have played very convincing roles without having experienced anything close in real life to what they're acting out on stage or film. Acting professionals are ideal people to help us learn to adapt our behavior and to thereby increase our CQ Action.

3.   MAKE TABOOS TABOO

Eliminate the behaviors that are most taboo in a culture you regularly encounter. Most people are forgiving of unintentional blunders when it comes to cross-cultural behavior. But it goes a long way when you avoid some of the basic offenses in the cultures you most often encounter.

The many tips offered in some books about the colors you should avoid or the inappropriate ways to greet people are helpful, but they can quickly become overwhelming. If you're doing extensive work with one culture, take the time to learn these specific things. However, most of us who move in and out of a lot of different cultures should find out what the major taboos are for cultures you most regularly encounter. Then keep your antenna up to discover other taboos you should avoid.

For example, it's a good rule of thumb to simply avoid handing people something with your left hand, since that's a highly offensive behavior in many cultures around the world. Avoid extended eye contact with the opposite sex unless you're certain it's appropriate for the individual and culture you're encountering. Pay attention to status and hierarchy, and let the person with higher status lead the way on the verbal and nonverbal interactions you have.

Robert's reference to the Christmas party could offend all kinds of people who come from different religious backgrounds, Sana included. Shaking her hand when they first met is also a taboo for many Muslim women. Robert can't be expected to know all these things but will be a more effective leader if he learns some of the basics and comes up with some behavioral strategies to follow the lead of culturally different people he meets.

The bestselling book *Kiss, Bow, or Shake Hands* is a great resource to keep on your shelf.[3] You can quickly look up the protocols for business and social interaction for more than sixty countries. In many cases, you'll be in the midst of a cross-cultural encounter with no advanced warning so you can't whip out a

ACTION

book and look up the taboos. Do the best you can, and then afterward, educate yourself and keep building your repertoire of behaviors so that you know which taboos to avoid. Here are a few taboos worth avoiding almost anywhere, since they are potentially offensive in so many cultures.

- Never photograph or touch a religious symbol (e.g., Buddha statute) without permission.

- Don't use your left hand to give a person something.

- Don't touch someone on the head.

- Don't touch your feet or put them up on furniture.

- Don't ask what someone's income is.

- Don't cuss or swear. What might seem innocent or appropriate in your context might be offensive elsewhere.

- Never initiate touch with the opposite sex.

- Avoid telling jokes or trying too hard to be humorous. It rarely translates cross-culturally.

- Avoid all ethnic slurs and jokes.

- Don't assume someone shares your views about politics, sexuality, religion, and so on.

Even this brief list plays out so differently in lots of places. And most taboos are culturally specific. For example, some cultures are very comfortable discussing age or personal income levels, but there are so many places where it is considered taboo that you're safer just not going there unless the other individual does. You can practice avoiding these behaviors even at home. If using both hands equally is fine in your culture, try going this next week without handing anyone anything with your left hand. Then pick another behavior that might not be offensive at home but try avoiding it for a week, just for practice.

ACTION

4. USE BASIC VOCABULARY

Language is a strategy that cuts through all four CQ capabilities, but it's most relevant to CQ Knowledge (studying a language) and CQ Action (using the language). There's no substitute for being fluent in a language to have the utmost effectiveness interacting, but that simply isn't possible for all the cultures we encounter.

For the cultures we most frequently encounter where we don't speak the language, many of the day-to-day issues and needs can be communicated with a core set of phrases and body language. This minimal vocabulary approach is very useful when you don't speak the language. Here's a list of crucial phrases worth learning to speak in other languages:

- Please

- Thank you

- Sorry

- Yes

- No

- Good

- Not good

- Hello

- Goodbye

- How much and too much (these two, used with a calculator or a piece of paper for writing numbers, are especially helpful when you're shopping)

- Come here

- Go there

ACTION

- Doesn't work (used in combination with pointing or handing)

- The word for your favorite beverage (water, beer, Coke)

- The word for something common to eat (rice, fish, meat, noodles)

- The word for a place to sleep (bed, room, hostel)

- Toilet

It's so much easier to speak a word or phrase than a complete sentence, and these words cover a lot of ground. For example, "Doesn't work," serves a multitude of situations. When you're in your hotel room, point to the empty toilet paper holder—"doesn't work" means there is no toilet paper and you want some. On the train, point to the train ticket and say, "Doesn't work," and the conductor will find your seat or compartment. At the laundry, point to the missing button and say, "Doesn't work," and someone will help you.[4]

I try to learn these phrases when I travel, no matter how short my visit. And if I can't learn them, I write them down and keep them with me. Learning a language is the key to getting a grip on a culture—but this strategy is better than nothing.

5. TRY NEW VOCAL SOUNDS

Language is the most significant part of our verbal behavior, but there are other important verbal actions to consider adapting, too. Most of us use a variety of vocalizations as part of our communication, probably without even realizing it.

For example, in the midst of conversation, many of us use fillers like "hmm," "uh-huh," clicking your tongue, or sucking in your breath. Or it might be the simple repetition of a word like "right," "got it," "sure, sure," or "can." Pick one of these that you use all the time and try eliminating it during a conversation. Or choose one you don't often use and try it out.

Another way to use this strategy is to think about your volume when you speak. How can you vary your volume to express different meanings? In many cultures, loud talking means power and authority and soft implies you lack confidence. Of course, it might mean just the opposite in another culture. For now, the purpose of this strategy is to just become comfortable with varying your volume when you talk. Try it during interpersonal conversations as well as in public speaking and see what occurs. Robert, like many African American men in the corporate context, has learned to soften his natural volume to avoid being perceived as a threatening, "angry black man."

Even when the same language is spoken, such as English, there's a great deal of variety in how words are pronounced. There are many variations in the way English is spoken in Australia as compared to India or Canada. And many differences exist even within the same countries, such as the varied dialects heard across the United Kingdom or throughout regions of the United States.

There are also some important differences that exist among English speakers, such as the way consonants are pronounced. For example, the United States usually uses a very hard "r" as compared to many English-speaking regions that use a much softer "r." Think of the way *park* is pronounced in New York vs. in Singapore. As insignificant as this might seem, strong assumptions can be formed about you based on these kinds of verbal behaviors. Try using a variety of verbal approaches to expand your options when you interact with someone from a different culture. You'll need to use the other capabilities of CQ to know whether you should actually adjust your pronunciation, but at least work on being able to do so if and when the situation calls for it.

Even though Sana and Haani have grown up in the United States, they're a real combination of their parents' Middle Eastern cultures and the mainstream American culture. Ensuring that Haani is comfortable with Robert would be an important value to many individuals coming from an Arab American culture. The phone conversation between Robert and Sana is awkward because cross-cultural differences are often felt more profoundly with the absence of any visual cues. Many Americans (myself included!) find it difficult to talk to someone when there are no verbal sounds to indicate that they're tracking with you (e.g., "uh-huh"). But individuals from many cultures find that kind of verbal behavior rude and distracting. Over time, you'll gain a broadened repertoire of social skills that you can draw on for a variety of cross-cultural interactions.

6. SLOW DOWN

I have two speeds: fast and faster. So this is a hard strategy for me. But I've learned the value of slowing down to enhance my CQ Action. A slower, more rhythmic pace allows us to deepen our insights and to simultaneously become more effective among the many individuals and cultures that aren't nearly as concerned with efficiency and accomplishment as people like me are. Effectively adjusting our behavior is more likely to happen when we slow down.

This particularly applies to our rate of speech. You may need to practice speaking more slowly and deliberately when interacting cross-culturally. Don't go overboard. We're not talking about speaking really loudly and slowly to someone from another culture. That's insulting. But when interacting with people whose dialect is different from ours or for whom our language isn't their primary language, we need to slow down our rate of speech. It's excruciatingly painful for me to speak slowly, particularly when I'm giving a presentation about something where I have a great deal of passion. But a simple way to enhance our CQ Action is to slow things down a bit. Not only does it enhance our effectiveness in the moment, but it also strengthens our overall CQ.

For many of us, our lives are predicated on an irrational compulsion for speed — we rush to work, we rush through meals, we multitask when we're hanging out with friends. This might make our lives feel more streamlined, but it doesn't make our lives happier or more fulfilling. Unless you learn to pace and savor your daily experiences (even your work commutes and your noontime meals), you'll be cheating your days out of small moments of leisure, discovery, and joy. And a constant, frenetic pace impedes an ability to adapt accordingly in the various cultural situations we encounter.

ACTION

7. PUT YOURSELF IN A PLACE OF NEED

Suzanne, an American expatriate working in France, discovered the importance of how she framed a request when she'd go shopping in Paris. Suzanne was fluent in French, but that didn't mitigate the challenges she felt in communicating. Early on during her sojourn in France, she couldn't seem to get beyond her perception that French people disliked Americans in general. Whenever she asked for something specific of a shopkeeper, such as, "Where can I find the lipstick?" she received a curt, abrupt response. One day, a French friend suggested, "Try starting with something like this when you walk into the store: 'Could you help me with a problem?' And if they say 'Yes'—which they more than likely will—then ask for help finding the lipstick." Suzanne tried it and couldn't believe how it seemed to change the disposition of the people waiting on her compared to her previous approach. She was now posturing herself as someone in need rather than coming in and making demands. She began to apply the same kinds of strategies with her colleagues and subordinates at work. She was amazed how this simple adjustment altered the way her requests were received.

Try to learn how to say the following in the language used in places you travel: "I'm sorry. I don't speak _____. Do you speak English?" The primary reason for this phrase is to posture yourself as one in need, rather than one making a demand. Think about how differently this communicates than when we just march up and ask, "Does anyone here speak English?" After all, if you're in Thailand, why should they speak English? You're the guest. Even a small effort to demonstrate that you realize it's your ignorance that's putting you at a disadvantage rather than vice versa goes a long way in motivating others to help you.

Here are a few examples to get you started. There are several online tools that can help you with the pronunciation, such as http://www.forvo.com/languages.

ACTION

Arabic

Ana aasaf. La atakellem al'arabiyya. Hel tatakellem
alingleeziyya?

Cantonese

Um-ho-yee-see. Ngo-umsick-gong-gwong-dung-wa.
Nay sick-um-sick gong yingmun.

Dutch

Ik betreur. Ik maak je geen woord Nederlands. Denkt u
maar Engels spreken?

German

Es tut mir leid. Ich spreche kein Deutsch. Sprechen
Sie Englisch?

French

Je, suis désolé. Je ne parle pas de français. Parlez-vous
l'anglais ?

Hindi

Maaf karein. Main Hindi nahin jaanta. Kya aap Angrezi
jaante hain?

Italian

Mi dispiace. Io non parlo italiano. Lei parla inglese?

Japanese

Gomen nasai. Nihongo shaberaremasen.
Ego shaberaremasuka?

Mandarin

Dui bu qi. Wo bu hui shuo Pu Tong Hua. Ni hui shuo
Ying yu ma?

Portuguese

Sinto muito, mas não falo Português. Você fala Inglês

Spanish

Perdón. No hablo español. ¿Habla Usted inglés?

Worst case, even saying the phrase in English, "I'm sorry, I don't speak _____. Do you speak English?" is much better than just blurting out, "Do you speak English?"

Simply understanding some basic shifts in language can make all the difference in achieving our objectives, whether it's to purchase lipstick or to launch a full-orbed initiative.[5]

8.   JOIN A MULTICULTURAL TEAM

Many of the strategies throughout each of these chapters are better accomplished when they include the perspective of other individuals. Surrounding yourself with other people can help you think better, and it enables you to see situations differently by looking through the eyes of others. For example, it's difficult to reframe circumstances realistically all by ourselves (a strategy from Chapter 5). But with the help of peers from various cultures, it's easier to do so. Collaborative efforts are most beneficial when they include culturally diverse members.

When you work with people from various cultures, you begin to observe a lot of the variations that exist in speech acts—the way you communicate. Whether it be apologies, expressions of gratitude, making requests directly or indirectly, knowing how to say "no" and how to respond when someone offers to "pay the bill," these are all things best learned through hands-on experiences in multicultural groups. Seek out experiences to work on projects that involve doing so with people from various cultures. Notice how differently each of you on a multicultural team approach conflict, make requests, apologize, compliment each other, and so on. And as you gain trust with each other, discuss some of these differences and ask questions such as, "What's the best response when someone won't let me pay the bill at a restaurant?" Then ask someone else. This will help you become more adaptable for a variety of cultural contexts.

Join or convene a group or team made up of individuals from a diversity of cultural backgrounds. Individuals who are part of multicultural teams are more likely to have higher CQ Action than those who are simply part of homogenous teams.[6] Culturally diverse groups offer you the opportunity to observe the behavior of culturally different individuals in the same context.

ACTION

The challenge with this strategy is that most adults gravitate toward people like them. We usually seek friends with similar tastes, beliefs, and interests. But in doing so, we miss out on so much. As you pursue relationships with individuals who see the world differently than you do, you have a profound edge in growing your CQ Action.

ACTION

BACK AT THE OFFICE

A little effort from both Robert and Sana to adapt their behavior could make their interactions much less awkward and provide a greater degree of clarity in their communication with each other. This is difficult during any cross-cultural interaction, but it's particularly hard over the phone, where nonverbal cues can't be directly observed. Robert's off-handed comment about Sana helping him add to the diversity mix at the office is primarily meant as a joke and as a way of lightening up their conversation, but humor rarely works cross-culturally, especially through telecommunication.

It's a tricky balance because if Robert overcompensates for how he thinks he should communicate to Sana given her different cultural background, it could be insulting to her. But thinking about how his words and talkative style might impact the way Sana hears him would be advantageous for both of them.

Sana doesn't have to use all kinds of vocalizations ("uh-huh," "sure" "yeah") if that's uncomfortable for her. But she should understand that many U.S. professionals lean upon these kinds of cues to demonstrate understanding, so some way of offering feedback would enhance her communication with Robert.

In an increasingly diverse workplace, Robert should be sensitive about referring to a company gathering as a "Christmas party." But Sana may also need to realize that he might not be intentionally trying to offend her or asking her to deny her faith simply by calling the holiday party a Christmas party. Notice that we want to see both individuals adapt some aspects of their behavior rather than assuming the responsibility is fully on one of them.

It's risky for Robert to use such a direct approach with the Middle Eastern executives, particularly when asking whether he should be concerned about dishonesty and corruption. At face value, it appears it didn't harm the negotiations, but only time will tell whether the company feels like the question brought shame upon them and eroded trust. A little effort to adapt our behavior will allow us to be more effective, honorable, and respectful.

ACTION

INCREASING YOUR CQ ACTION

Cultural blunders are inevitable, and most people are pretty for-giving of someone not knowing exactly how to behave in a culture that isn't their own. But an intentional effort to adapt and flex in ways that enhance understanding and cooperation will go a long way in helping us succeed in multicultural situations.

Identify two strategies you can begin using to enhance your CQ.

☐ 1. Develop a repertoire of social skills.		
☐ 2. Be an actor.	Nonverbal	
☐ 3. Make taboos taboo.		
☐ 4. Use basic vocabulary.		
☐ 5. Try new vocal sounds.	Verbal	
☐ 6. Slow down.		
☐ 7. Put yourself in a place of need.		
☐ 8. Join a multicultural team.	Speech Arts	

Which one will you try first? When?

ACTION

PART III

CONCLUDING THOUGHTS

The previous four chapters were devoted to drilling down into very specific ways to improve the four capabilities of CQ. But I want to conclude with a big-picture view of cultural intelligence and its associated strengths for helping you succeed.

The concluding material highlights several key strengths embedded in the cultural intelligence approach. You'll see how many organizations are leveraging these strengths, including an air transport company, a youth travel organization, a university, and the Canadian military. Finally, there are some concluding exercises to help you pull together your action plan for improving your CQ.

CHAPTER **7**

THE POWER OF CQ

I'm an eternal optimist. I believe anyone can change. And I'm driven by the crazy idea that the world can truly become a better place. This isn't blind idealism. I've seen it happen again and again—one interaction at a time—as people discover that "different" doesn't have to equal threatening or bad.

First and foremost, I've seen this in myself. I've moved from a pretty myopic perspective on the world to a broadened appreciation for diversity. Some of the changes have come slowly and painfully and others more quickly and easily. And our research on cultural intelligence has proven that everyone can improve their CQ. Granted, increased CQ comes more easily to some than others. But a desire to increase your CQ, combined with a plan to use some of the strategies covered in the last several chapters, is proven to strengthen your CQ. And increased CQ allows each of us to make the world a better place.

The skeptics roll their eyes. People have been feuding forever. Tribalism and ethnocentric behavior are common vices across all people and times. But humanity also has an unusual track record for changing history. CQ is rooted in the fundamental belief that people can change. You. Me. Everyone.

The power of CQ lies in its ability to foster transformation. There are several strengths associated with the overall nature of cultural intelligence. Let's take a closer look at them.

INTEGRATION

One of the most significant discoveries from our research on CQ is the importance of all four capabilities. One without the others can derail you. I've encouraged you to focus on the CQ capability where you scored lowest on the CQ assessment. But eventually, we have to get back to thinking about all four capabilities together because excessive attention on one CQ capability at the expense of others may actually result in increased cultural ignorance. All four CQ capabilities are interrelated.

If you have a deep understanding of cultural differences (high CQ Knowledge), it doesn't mean you can apply your knowledge to developing an effective plan (CQ Strategy). Or if you're very confident in your ability to work in a different culture (high CQ Drive), but have very little cultural understanding (CQ Knowledge), your confidence could actually get you into trouble rather than helping you.

Here's how this might look practically. A traveling business-woman with high CQ Drive and Action might fully engage in a lot of hands-on experiences as she travels across cultures—seeing the sights, eating the local foods, and exploring things off the beaten path. However, without high CQ Knowledge and Strategy, she won't fully learn from these experiences because she lacks the observational skills and conceptual understanding to transform her experience into knowledge that can guide her in future cross-cultural encounters. In a similar way, someone with high CQ

Knowledge and Strategy who lacks CQ Drive may gain cultural insights through books and observations but refrain from seeking real interactions that provide more holistic experiences and deeper learning that can be applied to future interactions and work.[1]

The good news is, given the interrelationship of the four CQ capabilities, by giving attention to one, you may simultaneously enhance another. For example, gaining a stronger understanding of cultural differences via CQ Knowledge can help you feel more in control by learning more about the culture. The planning that is part of CQ Strategy also helps you develop a sense of control and equilibrium. And the repertoire of behaviors gained through CQ Action gives you more options for how to engage with a diversity of individuals. Gaining some control over your circumstances in cross-cultural situations will enhance your CQ Drive—and quite possibly, the other CQ capabilities, too. The four distinct yet integrated capabilities of CQ are a crucial part of the CQ difference.

PROGRESSION

Another strength lies in the developmental nature of cultural intelligence. CQ isn't a static or fixed capability. It's based on the premise that our capabilities in cultural intelligence are continually morphing and progressing. The four capabilities don't always develop in one particular order. It can be helpful, however, to think about them as four steps toward enhanced overall cultural intelligence. The most likely progression of the four CQ capabilities is shown in Figure 7-1.

Figure 7-1 CQ capability progression.

Step 1: CQ Drive gives us the energy and self-confidence to pursue the needed cultural understanding and planning.

Step 2: CQ Knowledge provides us with an understanding of basic cultural cues.

Step 3: CQ Strategy allows us to draw on our cultural understanding so we can plan and interpret what's going on in diverse contexts.

Step 4: CQ Action provides us with the ability to engage in effective flexible leadership across cultures.

Then it's back to Step 1. As others respond to our behavior, the cycle starts over. Our experiences (CQ Action) shape our motivation (CQ Drive) for future interactions.

The four-step cycle is something that can be applied at a macro level in thinking through your overall development in CQ. Or it's a cycle you can run through on the fly when preparing for a cross-cultural encounter. For example, imagine Sana using this prior to her first interview with Robert:

Step 1: CQ Drive
What's my motivation for adapting to the culture of Indianapolis, this company's culture, and the culture of my potential boss? (In part—to get a job!)

Step 2: CQ Knowledge
What do I need to know about these cultures? (e.g., What's their experience with Arab Americans? What's the dominant religious subculture here?)

Step 3: CQ Strategy
What's my plan? (e.g., What questions should I ask?
How can I dispel the assumptions that might be made
about me as a Muslim?)

Step 4: CQ Action
Can I adapt accordingly? (Should I shake Robert's hand?
How should I respond to the question of how long I've
lived in the United States?)

A company can also use this four-step process to think about
a firm-wide initiative. Robert's company can use it to think about
the potential acquisition by the Middle Eastern company:

Step 1: CQ Drive
What's our motivation for understanding Middle Eastern
culture?

Step 2: CQ Knowledge
What do we need to understand about the cultures involved
to make a decision?

Step 3: CQ Strategy
What's our negotiating plan in light of the cultural
differences?

Step 4: CQ Action
How should we adapt while still retaining our core values
as a company?

This four-step progression of developing CQ is the primary
way I apply CQ to leaders in my book *Leading with Cultural
Intelligence*. Nobody ever "arrives" at perfect CQ. It's an ongoing
journey. But as we continue to work through these four steps in
lots of different scenarios, adapting to various cultural situations
will become more natural.

TENSION

Intercultural work is full of paradox and contradiction. An ability to hold things in tension is absolutely essential for effective adaptation cross-culturally.

• Be yourself. Adapt to local cultures.

• Retain your brand. Adjust to local tastes.

• Fight corruption. Respect cultural norms.

• Unify your team. Embrace diversity.

• We're all the same. We're all different.

The cultural intelligence model not only allows for holding contradictions in tension but also creates a way to lean into the insights and opportunities that can be created by tension. Tension is something we often resist, but tension doesn't have to be bad. Think about your favorite movies. They inevitably involve stories with some sort of trouble and conflict for various characters that needs to be resolved. Tension makes stories more interesting and forces creativity. In multicultural settings, tension often develops as people from various cultures and perspectives become intertwined. This can derail a project and relationship or it can be the very thing that enriches it. CQ draws on the strengths of tension as a creative force for innovation.

The growth of multiculturalism and globalization brings us rising levels of complexity and nuance. The ability to hold tension is absolutely essential. Fundamentalism—strict adherence to one's view of the world as the only right way—is essentially a refusal to live in tension. It's an unwillingness to even consider a different perspective, much less reformulate one's view. In contrast, a culturally intelligent posture holds in tension a commitment to personal values and beliefs with an appreciation and respect for other's values and beliefs, even when they conflict with your own. And this is more than just tolerance. It will probably mean accommodating for some shifts in your personal values and beliefs.

As noted several times, CQ includes yet transcends the traditional intercultural approaches that emphasize comparing people from different national cultures. These simplistic generalizations of how people behave based on their countries of origin can be helpful but must be held loosely in order to see each individual in light of who they are personally. CQ promotes this kind of complex thinking, which is "evoked by situations where two contradictory statements may be both true or where a statement may be true and not true at the same time, or when formal logic remains insufficient."[2]

The culturally intelligent individual holds in tension the assets and liabilities of hierarchical, top-down leadership vs. egalitarian, flat leadership models. He or she appreciates the strengths and weakness of love marriages vs. arranged marriages. Both approaches can be positive and both can become negative. CQ allows us to hold polarities in tension rather than simply trying to reduce or dismiss the tension. CQ will help you embrace the tension of the opposites.

REFLECTION

To a strong degree, the power of CQ also lies in its use of reflective thinking. Over the last several years, a great deal has been made about harnessing the power of reflection. Just as a mirror allows us to adjust our external appearance, reflecting on our thoughts and experiences is a key way of adjusting our internal assumptions and behaviors. Reflection is a skill that helps us structure meaning around our experiences. As human beings, we can't stop thinking. Every moment is filled with all kinds of impressions. As we sort through the barrage of impressions that come our way daily, we order some into the background and bring others into sharper focus. This occurs through reflective thinking.

Donald Schon is one of the foremost experts on the role of reflection in the workplace. Schon looked at how professionals think in the course of their everyday work. In his study of the way architects, psychotherapists, engineers, town planners, and managers operated on the job, he describes the process as *reflection-in-action*.

Professionals can't just problem solve. They also have to do *problem setting*. Problem solving asks, "How do we build this?" Problem setting asks, "What is the right thing to build?" The goal isn't just to find answers, but to form hypotheses that help explain a problem in the first place. This is a highly generative activity that requires a synthesis of reflection and action (another tension!). Problem setting is unlikely to come on the fly but only through the kind of reflective discipline elevated by the CQ approach. Reflective practice is most strongly connected to CQ Strategy—learning how to interpret observations and plan in light of them. But it's woven throughout the overall CQ model as well.

CQ highlights the importance of reflection before and after an intercultural encounter *and* reflection in the midst of the encounter. Schon argues that alongside reflection-in-action, there is also a place for ancillary, outside-of-practice learning that enhances a practitioner's capacity to think in doing.[3] Working and relating in multicultural contexts requires solving unexpected problems with unpredictable solutions. We need to learn to reflect in the midst of action and create space to step aside from our constant movement to contemplate, reflect, and prepare for future action.

Many of our twenty-first-century cultures place little value on slowing down to take the time to reflect, particularly in the business context. But cultural intelligence is integrally connected to a disciplined effort to reflect in the midst of and outside of our frenzied multicultural work.

INSPIRATION: SUCCESS STORIES

One of the things I love about being part of the cultural intelligence movement is the variety of inspiring individuals and organizations I get to encounter. One day I'm working with a large pharmaceutical company that is wrestling with how its increasingly global operation fits with its conservative, Midwest U.S. roots. The next day I'm with the U.S. Department of Justice thinking about how CQ helps it promote justice and apprehend enemies without perpetuating ethnic stereotypes. And yet another day I'm interacting with a charitable organization working in Haiti.

I have little interest in academic research that doesn't make a difference in the world. But individuals and organizations around the world are using the findings from CQ research to improve their lives and to make the world a better place. Entrepreneurs, teachers, parents, and artists are incorporating CQ into their work. Colleen, a business coach, finds that CQ is the ideal complement to the psychological tools she uses to help expats assimilate into a new culture (or to reenter their own culture when they get back home).

Rising Indian rock star Wilbur Sargunaraj is using his concert platforms to inspire and teach fans about CQ so that they not only tolerate different cultures but embrace cultural differences and learn from them. Habib, a CEO of a multimillion-dollar Middle Eastern firm, is using CQ to improve the way his company does mergers and acquisitions. Florence, a relief and development worker in South Africa, has described CQ as the single greatest learning tool she's encountered to help her work successfully with culturally diverse NGOs and her fellow Africans across southern Africa.

Thousands of organizations around the world share inspiring reports of how CQ is helping them in a variety of ways, including human resource policies, marketing initiatives, negotiation practices, and new business opportunities. But the most inspiring success stories come from organizations that are integrating CQ all throughout their work. Many groups are doing so but here are a few specific examples.

The International Air Transport Association

The International Air Transport Association (IATA) is headquartered in Geneva and Montreal, but its personnel represent 140 different nationalities and work in 74 countries. IATA is the primary voice of the airline industry to government and media. It provides technical support and training to the 230 airlines that are members of IATA. Despite the international breadth of IATA's staff and work, the corporate ethos of the organization has traditionally been biased toward Western ideas and practices, with limited appreciation of important fast-growing markets in other parts of the world. IATA faces the same problems many other organizations around the world have faced:

● How do we operate in markets we don't fully understand?

● Where do we find leaders able to grow local business, communicate with headquarters, and manage local teams effectively while implementing global processes, initiatives, and strategies?

The traditional solution to these problems has been to send out experts from the corporate headquarters (Western expats) to set up and manage branch offices around the world. In more recent years, companies are sending Singaporean-born Chinese or British-born Indians to work in places like China and India because of a belief that managers with this kind of bicultural background can uniquely bridge both worlds.

IATA has taken a different approach by developing what it calls the I-Lead Program—Intercultural Leadership Engagement and Development. Each year, IATA's top management team selects twenty high-potential individuals from its workforce to be in I-Lead. Half the group are from traditional markets like Western Europe and North America with individualistic and low power-distance national cultures. The other half are from emerging markets that feature collectivist and high power-distance cultures such as China and India.[4]

Each of the twenty I-Lead participants is paired up with one other person in the group to co-lead a team of junior, high-potential employees in different locations and work on a real-life business project that is relevant to IATA. Essentially, ten IATA teams around the world are being co-led by one Western and one non-Western leader who work extensively on a set of deliverables in addition to their regular job responsibilities. Each pair of participants is assigned one senior executive as sponsor and one as coach to support and guide them along this program. At the end of the six-month period, the teams present their project results and cross-cultural lessons learned to IATA's top executive team. The business innovations that have emerged from this program have translated into increased profitability for IATA and its member airlines. Have you noticed the move away from "swiping" your boarding pass when you board the plane to scanning bar codes—a more efficient way to board passengers and collect the necessary data? Airlines and airports around the world are implementing bar code boarding. This idea emerged from an I-Lead project.

All the I-Lead participants meet together from around the world for one week at the beginning of the program and again at the end. The launch workshop is held in an important emerging market and is attended by the CEO. Everyone participates in a *CQ Multi-Rater Assessment*, which includes both a self-assessment of their CQ capabilities and assessment by a select number of coworkers and a supervisor. When they come together, they receive their feedback report and talk about how to interpret the findings. And they experience a week of experiential learning about culture and its impact on how they lead on behalf of IATA around the world. In addition to pairing up with another I-Lead participant to manage a team together, each participant will be teaching cultural intelligence to their project team back at their home office, which, in turn, enhances the degree to which they internalize the material.

Guido Gianasso, IATA's vice president of Human Capital, reports that this program has been one of its most profitable leadership development initiatives. A recently completed empirical study on the more than 200 past I-LEAD participants supports the conclusion that the program has significantly improved all four of their CQ capabilities. The program has helped IATA build bridges across different cultures and has played a direct role in the growth of the business in emerging markets.

Canadian Armed Forces

Military leaders have been discussing the importance of cultural understanding and adaptability as long as any group has. But the Canadian military's experience in Afghanistan is playing a key role in its renewed focus on the importance of culture and CQ. The Canadian Forces are integrating CQ throughout their operational, strategic, and tactical imperatives. Defense researcher and retired Lieutenant-Commander Karen Davis writes, "CQ is an essential contributor to the ability to determine adversarial intent; to work effectively across joint, interagency, multinational and public domains (JIMP), to access and exercise whole of government (WOG) approaches, and to negotiate the demands of interrelated defence, diplomacy, and development (3D) objectives."[5]

A great deal of CQ is needed by the coalition forces working in Afghanistan. For example, many Afghan village women are seen only by their family members. They rarely leave their homes, and when they do, they cover their faces so no man except their husband can see them. So when male coalition soldiers march into villages and barge into homes to search for explosive devices, there's little cooperation—not to mention a huge insult and offense to the locals.

Canadian Forces are changing this approach. When possible, female soldiers go into the village to form bonds with the women and children. They talk to them about education and explain how the coalition effort will provide opportunity for Afghan children to go to school and have opportunities rather than joining up with insurgency armies. In describing this experience, Canadian Corporal Melissa Gagnon said, "The [Afghan women] actually smiled when we came in. It seems like there may not have been women [soldiers] here before."[6] When female soldiers aren't available, their male counterparts are talking with village men first so that the Afghan women have time to cover their faces before the men come into their homes to do searches.

This more culturally intelligent strategy treats the Afghans with respect and dignity. And it's also a more successful strategy in terms of the military mission. But it doesn't stop here. As noted by Karen Davis, "The development of CQ across the Canadian Forces is dependent upon reflection, dialogue, continuous learning, lessons learned, and most importantly, the application of adaptable and innovative critical analyses to cultural challenges and dilemmas."[7]

People to People

The People to People movement was begun in 1956 by U.S. President Dwight Eisenhower, who believed that direct interaction between ordinary citizens around the world could promote cultural understanding and world peace. Today, Eishenhower's mission is carried out by People to People Student Ambassadors and the People to People Ambassador Programs. More than 400,000 Americans have traveled with People to People Ambassador Programs to seven continents around the world. The organization focuses primarily on using educational travel to develop cultural intelligence and social consciousness in children and adolescents. Youth travel on People to People delegations led by classroom teachers who volunteer their time because of their commitment to nurture CQ in youth. They believe CQ will enhance young people's opportunities personally and their ability to make the world a better place.

Cultural understanding and engagement have been core values for People to People Ambassador Programs long before CQ became a formalized concept. For over fifty years, the organization has been a leader in doing educational travel in a socially conscious way. Today, the executives at the company are integrating the CQ research and model into their work from top to bottom. They don't believe that sending individuals overseas automatically translates into improved CQ. Instead, they intentionally design the program to enhance CQ:

- The process begins with a careful selection process in light of a young person's motivation for traveling abroad (CQ Drive).

- Next, leaders and delegates are prepared through a series of online and in-person training modules (CQ Knowledge).

- Leaders then prepare their delegates by giving them journals and providing specific prompts to help them become more aware of and alert to cultural differences (CQ Strategy).

- Itineraries are developed with the use of a local guide to think about how to best behave while interacting with the various cultures encountered (CQ Action).

As well as rooting the overall program and experience in this developmental approach, each day of a delegation's itinerary incorporates these elements as well. For example, a group preparing to visit the Vatican will consider the following:

- What's our motivation for learning more about the Vatican (CQ Drive)?

- What do we need to learn before we go and while we're there (CQ Knowledge)?

- How should we plan to behave? To what should we remain alert (CQ Strategy)?

• What behavior should we adapt in order to respect the cultural norms (CQ Action)?

People to People Ambassador Programs look at how CQ informs their programs. In addition, the leadership is using it throughout the organization as a whole. Individuals in the program office are being assessed and trained in cultural intelligence, students who participate in the overseas trips are being assessed in CQ before and after they travel, and the educators who lead the trips are being trained in how to maximize the educational trips as a way to enhance the CQ of students over the long haul. In addition, the company supports an online forum, www.societyforglobalcitizens.com/, to foster ongoing interaction about issues related to cultural intelligence and global citizenship long after a trip abroad.

Nanyang Technological University, Singapore

Nanyang Technological University (NTU), a leading research university in Singapore, is often referred to as the MIT of the East. It's no surprise that the business school has integrated teaching and assessment of CQ throughout its undergraduate and graduate programs, given that some of the leading researchers of CQ teach there. Undergraduate students in the business school work together in multicultural teams, assess one another's CQ, and create a plan for developing their CQ in the areas where they need it most.

MBA students at Nanyang Business School travel abroad on short-term study missions to places like Vietnam or Ireland. The students are paired up with classmates from different cultures (an easy task given the diversity at the university), and they're tasked with setting up meetings with businesses based in the country they'll visit. They have a series of assignments to apply CQ as they encounter multinational firms, and they develop a long-term CQ development plan for themselves and their work in business. The business school draws heavily on CQ assessments to show accrediting bodies like the Association to Advance Collegiate Schools of Business (AACSB) how the university's programs enhance students' global competency.

Nanyang Business School's commitment to cultural intelligence is one of the things attributed to putting it among the top hundred business schools in the world and among the top ten schools in the region.[8] CQ is being adopted at other schools and departments of the university as well. Singapore's National Institute of Education is based at NTU and is equipping the nation's teachers with CQ as a key set of capabilities needed for twenty-first-century classrooms. And plans are under way for every incoming freshman to take a course in CQ. Additional expressions of CQ exist throughout the administration of the university and in numerous other departments.

*　*　*

Hundreds of other individuals and organizations are incorporating the findings of CQ into their work. Large companies such as Bank of America, Barclays, and IBM, government agencies such as the U.S. Department of Justice and the Swiss legislature, universities such as University of Minnesota, Georgetown, and Stanford, and charitable organizations such as the Red Cross and World Vision are just a few of the organizations tapping into the benefits associated with the CQ difference.

APPLICATION

The greatest strength of CQ lies in its application to our lives, relationships, and work in today's global, interdependent world. I have little interest in ideas that don't actually go anywhere. Throughout the book, I've been encouraging you to identify where you'll begin work to improve your CQ. Use the following questions to give you an overview of your CQ action plan.

CREATING YOUR CQ ACTION PLAN

Leverage Your Strengths

Circle your strongest CQ capability (based on your scores from the *CQ Self-Assessment*):

CQ Drive   CQ Knowledge
CQ Strategy   CQ Action

How can you leverage this strength?

_____

_____

What can you do next week to tap into this strength?

_____

_____

Manage Your Weaknesses

Circle your weakest CQ capability (based on your scores from the *CQ Self-Assessment*):

CQ Drive   CQ Knowledge
CQ Strategy   CQ Action

What can you do next week to address this weakness?

_____

_____

Strategies to Improve Your CQ

We've reviewed the following strategies for improving your CQ.

Circle the one or two strategies you'll begin using immediately.

Put an * next to the strategies you'll come back to in four to six weeks.

CQ Drive	CQ Knowledge
1. Face your biases.	1. Study culture up close.
2. Connect with existing interests.	2. Google smarter.
3. Scare yourself.	3. Improve your global awareness.
4. Visualize success.	4. Go to the movies or read a novel.
5. Reward yourself.	5. Learn about cultural values.
6. Recharge your batteries.	6. Explore your cultural identity.
7. Maintain control.	7. Study a new language.
8. Travel.	8. Seek diverse perspectives.
	9. Recruit a CQ coach.

CQ Strategy	CQ Action
1. Notice; don't respond.	1. Develop a repertoire of social skills.
2. Think widely.	2. Be an actor.
3. Focus deeply.	3. Make taboos taboo.
4. Journal.	4. Use basic vocabulary.
5. Plan social interactions.	5. Try new vocal sounds.
6. Manage expectations.	6. Slow down.
7. Create checklists.	7. Put yourself in a place of need.
8. Reframe a situation.	8. Join a multicultural team.
9. Test for accuracy.	
10. Ask better questions.	

MOVING FORWARD

We can't navigate today's globalized world using old maps. And it won't help to simply update the names and colors of our old maps. They were made for a different world. CQ gives us a new map for navigating the terrain of today's globalized world.

The CQ map includes some familiar features of previous maps such as learning about cultural values and studying a new language. But CQ transcends those features. Cultural intelligence is an integrative, progressive approach that prepares us for an onslaught of multicultural twists and turns. CQ calls us to be authentically true to our personal and organizational values while also learning to respect, defer, and learn from the values and concerns of others.

To improve your cultural intelligence is to embark on seeing the world in a whole new way. It's at times painful and even fear-invoking, but the rewards are well worth it. It's amazing what happens when we're willing to move beyond our differences to see one another first and foremost as human beings. Then, from our common bond as humans, we can learn from our differences. That's the power of CQ. That's the CQ difference.

EPILOGUE

The world has forever changed. Will you change with it? Will you be an agent of change? Or will you resist with despair, burnout, and exhaustion? Together—as we work hard to enhance our cultural intelligence—we can be catalysts for the most unlikely connections.

* * *

Imagine a liberal politician and a Tea Party activist engaging in respectful dialogue.

Imagine a Jewish family sharing a holiday getaway with a Palestinian family.

Imagine a CEO working with a hip-hop artist to reduce world hunger.

Imagine an ACLU advocate joining an evangelical pastor to promote justice.

* * *

Tolerance isn't enough. We have to move toward each other. We have to transcend and include our differences to collaboratively make the world a better place.

When you move toward people of difference while still remaining true to yourself, something powerful happens. Suddenly, you can't go along with the conversations at your family reunion about "those Muslims," the problem with "all the Chinese," or those "idiotic liberals" or "greedy conservatives." The simplistic categories of "us" vs. "them" won't work anymore, and that's good for all of us!

We've never had more opportunities to encounter people who see and experience the world differently than we do today. Embrace it. And discover the possibilities of seeing the world in a whole new way.

The One-Year Performance Review

Neither Robert nor Sana can believe they've been working together for a year now. Sana isn't very anxious about her performance review because she senses that Robert is very pleased with her work and she enjoys working with him. Haani isn't happy that she often brings work home, but he's grateful Robert and his wife, Ingrid, recently agreed to come have dinner with them. Who would have thought that Robert and Ingrid would be joining Sana and Haani as they break their Ramadan fast?

Robert and Ingrid are still as active and engaged in their Christian church as they were a year ago. But they find themselves more unnerved these days when they hear harsh, dogmatic statements made about Muslims—whether it be at church, on the news, or sitting in the soccer stands. Sana and Haani found a mosque where they go for their weekly Friday prayers, but there's something about Robert and Ingrid's unconventional approach to religion (at least through Sana and Haani's eyes) that's endearing to them.

Instead of selling the business unit to the Middle Eastern company, Robert's firm did a merger with the company. In just six months' time, it's become the most profitable line of business. Sana has been indispensable to the company in helping it interpret various e-mails that come in from the Middle Eastern partners. And Robert helps Sana understand some of what Haani is experiencing at the pharmaceutical company. Together, they're improving each others' lives, families, and the work of their company.

I look forward to seeing how your own multicultural experiences, combined with improving your CQ, have a similar effect on you, me, and the rest of the world. I'd love to hear your experiences. Visit me online at www.davidlivermore.com and share with me and others what you're learning about the CQ difference.

NOTES

Preface

1. Soon Ang and Linn Van Dyne, "Conceptualization of Cultural Intelligence" in *Handbook of Cultural Intelligence: Theory, Measurement, and Applications* (Armonk, NY: M.E. Sharpe, 2008), 10.

2. For those who care about such things, I've used the terms *cross-cultural, intercultural,* and *multicultural* synonymously throughout the book. Although technically *cross-cultural* traditionally refers to "two cultures interacting" and *intercultural* and *multicultural* refer to "multiple cultures interacting," I find it helps to use the terms interchangeably for this kind of writing.

Chapter 1: CQ for You

1. Siobhan Roth, "World Travelers," *National Geographic* July 2006, 25. Admittedly, there are some individuals who get more than one tourist visa in a year; therefore, 1 billion is a rough estimate. But there are also others who move across borders without getting a tourist visa. So ⅙ still seems like a fair estimate of the number of people in the world traveling internationally each year.

2. Claudia Deutsch, "GE: A General Store for Developing World," *International Herald Tribune*, July 18, 2005, 17.

3. Less Christie, "CNN, Census: U.S. Becoming More Diverse," http://money.cnn.com/2009/05/14/real_estate/rising_minorities/index.htm (accessed May 21, 2009).

4. Giovanni Bisignani, "Improved Profitability—But Europe Still Lags in the Red," International Air Transport Authority, http://www.iata.org/pressroom/pr/Pages/2010-09-21-02.aspx., September 19, 2010.

5. David Livermore, "Globalization Trends," a technical report created for the Global Learning Center, Grand Rapids, MI: September 2008.

6. Cheryl Tay, Mina Westman, and Audrey Chia, "Antecedents and Consequences of Cultural Intelligence Among Short-Term Business Travelers," in *Handbook of Cultural Intelligence: Theory, Measurement, and Applications* (Armonk, NY: M.E. Sharpe, 2008), 141.

7. Thomas Ruckstuhl, Ying-yi Hong, Soon Ang, and Chi-Yue Chiu, "The Culturally Intelligent Brain: Possible Neuroscience Foundation of Global Leadership," *Neuroleadership Journal* (forthcoming).

8. Gary Ferraro, *The Cultural Dimension of International Business,* 5th Ed. (Upper Saddle River, NJ: Prentice-Hall, 2006), 12.

9. Aimin Yan and Yadong Luo, *International Joint Ventures: Theory and Practice* (Armonk, NY: ME Sharpe, 2001), 32.

10. Soon Ang, Linn Van Dyne, and Mei Ling Tan, "Cultural Intelligence," in Robert J. Sternberg and Scott Barry Kaufman, eds. *Cambridge Handbook of Intelligence* (Cambridge, U.K.: Cambridge University Press, (forthcoming).

11. Soon Ang and Linn Van Dyne, "Conceptualization of Cultural Intelligence," in *Handbook of Cultural Intelligence: Theory, Measurement, and Applications* (Armonk, NY: M.E. Sharpe, 2008), 10.

12. Ibid.

13. Ibid.

14. Soon Ang, Linn Van Dyne, C. Koh, K. Y. Ng, K. J. Templer, C. Tay, and N. A. Chandrasekar, "Cultural Intelligence: Its Measurement and Effects on Cultural Judgment and Decision Making, Cultural Adaptation, and Task Performance," *Management and Organization Review* 3 (2007): 335–371.

15. L. Imai and M. J. Gelfand, "The Culturally Intelligent Negotiator: The Impact of Cultural Intelligence (CQ) on Negotiation Sequences and Outcomes," *Organizational Behavior and Human Decision Processes* 112: 83–98.

16. Grant McCracken, *Chief Culture Officer: How to Create a Living, Breathing Corporation* (New York: Basic Books, 2009), 148.

17. Soon Ang, Linn Van Dyne, and Mei Ling Tan, "Cultural Intelligence." In Robert J. Sternberg and Scott Barry Kaufman, eds. *Cambridge Handbook of Intelligence* (Cambridge, U.K.: Cambridge University Press (forthcoming).

18. Ibid.

19. Ibid.

20. Cheryl Tay, Mina Westman, and Audrey Chia, "Antecedents and Consequences of Cultural Intelligence Among Short-Term Business Travelers" in *Handbook of Cultural Intelligence: Theory, Measurement, and Applications* (Armonk, NY: M.E. Sharpe, 2008), 126ff.

21. David Livermore, "The Results of Cultural Intelligence," technical report for the Global Learning Center, Grand Rapids, MI, 2009.

22. Ibid.

23. Ibid.

24. Ibid.

25. Elie Wiesel, *Dawn* (New York: Hill and Wang, 2006), vii.

26. Ken Wilbur, *Boomeritis: A Novel That Will Set You Free* (Boston, Shambhala, 2002), 15.

27. Henry Cloud, *Integrity: The Courage to Meet the Demands of Reality* (New York: Collins, 2006), 242.

Chapter 2: Research Brief

1. Milton Bennett, "Towards Ethnorelativism: A Developmental Model of Intercultural Sensitivity," in R. Michael Paige, ed., *Education for the Intercultural Experience* (Yarmouth, ME: Intercultural Press, 1993) 21–71; Geert Hofstede, *Cultures and Organizations: Software of the Mind* (New York: McGraw-Hill, 1997); and Fons Trompenaars and Charles Hampden-Turner, *Riding the Waves of Culture: Understanding Diversity in Global Business* (New York: McGraw Hill, 2000).

2. M. J. Gelfand, L. Imai, and R. Fehr, "Thinking Intelligently About Cultural Intelligence: The Road Ahead," in S. Ang and L. Van Dyne, eds., *Handbook of Cultural Intelligence: Theory, Measurement, and Applications* (New York: M.E. Sharpe, 2008), 375.

3. Soon Ang, Linn Van Dyne, and Mei Ling Tan, "Cultural Intelligence," in Robert J. Sternberg and Scott Barry Kaufman, eds. *Cambridge Handbook of Intelligence* (Cambridge, U.K.: Cambridge University Press (forthcoming).

4. J. D. Mayer and P. Salovey, "What Is Emotional Intelligence?" in P. Salovey and D. Sluter, eds., *Emotional Development and Emotional Intelligence: Educational Applications* (New York: Basic Books, 1997), 3–31.

5. R. Thorndike and S. Stein, "An Evaluation of the Attempts to Measure Social Intelligence," *Psychological Bulletin* 34 (1937): 275–285.

6. R. J. Sternberg, and R. J. Wagner, "Practical Intelligence," in R. J. Sternberg, ed., *Handbook of Intelligence* (New York: Cambridge University Press, 2000), 380–395.

7. Chris Earley and Soon Ang, *Cultural Intelligence: Individual Interactions Across Cultures* (Stanford, CA: Stanford Press, 2003).

8. R. J. Sternberg and D. K. Detterman, eds., *What Is Intelligence? Contemporary Viewpoints on Its Nature and Definition* (Norwood, NJ: Ablex, 1986).

9. R. J. Sternberg, "A Framework for Understanding Conceptions of Intelligence," in R. J. Sternberg and D. K. Detterman, eds., *What Is Intelligence?* (Norwood, NJ: Ablex, 1986), 3–18.

10. Cultural Intelligence Scale (CQS), East Lansing, MI: Cultural Intelligence Center, LLC, 2005.

11. S. Ang, L. Van Dyne, C. K. S. Koh, K. Y. Ng, K. J. Templer, C. Tay, and N. A. Chandrasekar, "Cultural Intelligence: Its Measurement and Effects on Cultural Judgment and Decision Making, Cultural Adaptation, and Task Performance, *Management and Organization Review* 3 (2007): 335–371.

12. S. Ang, L. Van Dyne, and M. L. Tan, "Cultural Intelligence," in R. J. Sternberg and S. B. Kaufman, eds. *Cambridge Handbook of Intelligence* (Cambridge: Cambridge University Press, forthcoming).

13. S. Ang, L. Van Dyne, C. Koh, K. Y. Ng, K. J. Templer, C. Tay, and N. A. Chandrasekar, "Cultural Intelligence: Its Measurement and Effects on Cultural Judgment and Decision-Making, Cultural Adaptation, and Task Performance," *Management and Organization Review* 3, (2007): 340.

Chapter 3: CQ Drive

1. Linn Van Dyne and Soon Ang, "The Sub-Dimensions of the Four-Factor Model of Cultural Intelligence," Technical Report. Cultural Intelligence Center, 2008.

2. M. Goh, J. Koch, and S. Sanger, "Cultural Intelligence in Counseling Psychology," in Soon Ang and Linn Van Dyne, eds., *Handbook of Cultural Intelligence: Theory, Measurement, and Applications* (Armonk, NY: M.E. Sharpe, 2008), 41–54; Ibraiz Tarique and Riki Takeuchi, "Developing Cultural Intelligence: The Role of International Nonwork Experiences," in *Handbook of Cultural Intelligence: Theory, Measurement, and Applications* (Armonk, NY: M.E. Sharpe, 2008), 260, 264.

3. Soon Ang, Linn Van Dyne, and Mei Ling Tan, "Cultural Intelligence," in Robert J. Sternberg and Scott Barry Kaufman, eds. *Cambridge Handbook of Intelligence* (Cambridge, U.K.: Cambridge University Press, (forthcoming).

4. David Rock, *Your Brain at Work: Strategies for Overcoming Distraction, Regaining Focus, and Working Smarter All Day Long* (New York: Harper Collins, 2009), 65.

5. Klaus Templer, C. Tay, and N. A. Chandrasekar, "Motivational Cultural Intelligence, Realistic Job Preview, Realistic Living Conditions Preview, and Cross-Cultural Adjustment," *Group & Organization Management* 31, 1 (February 2006): 157.

6. Rock, 66.

7. G. Latham and E. Locke, "Employee Motivation," in Julian Barling and Cary Cooper, eds. *The SAGE Handbook of Organizational Behavior, Volume I, Micro Approaches* (Thousand Oaks, CA: SAGE, 2009), 320.

8. E. Berkman and M. D. Lieberman, "The Neuroscience of Goal Pursuit: Bridging Gaps Between Theory and Data," in G. Moskowitz and H. Grant, eds. *The Psychology of Goals* (New York: Guilford Press, 2009), 98–126.

9. Paulo Freire, *Pedagogy of the Oppressed* (New York: Continuum, 1997).

10. Rock, 36.

11. Ellen Langer, *Counterclockwise: Mindful Health and the Power of Possibility* (New York: Ballantine Books, 2009), 112–115.

12. Amy Arnsten, Prefrontal Cortical Networks, http://info.med.yale.edu/neurobio/arnsten/Research.html (accessed January 13, 2010).

13. David Rock, "Managing with the Brain in Mind," *Strategy and Business* (Autumn 2009), 56, http://www.strategy-business.com/article/ 09306? gko=5df7f&cid=enews20091013.

14. L. M. Shannon and T. M. Begley, "Antecedents of the Four-Factor Model of Cultural Intelligence," in Soon Ang and Linn Van Dyne, eds., *Handbook of Cultural Intelligence: Theory, Measurement, and Applications* (Armonk, NY: M.E. Sharpe, 2008), 41–54. And Ibraiz Tarique and Riki Takeuchi, "Developing Cultural Intelligence: The Role of International Nonwork Experiences," in *Handbook of Cultural Intelligence: Theory, Measurement, and Applications* (Armonk, NY: M.E. Sharpe, 2008), 56.

15. Efrat Shokef and Miriam Erez, "Cultural Intelligence and Global Identity in Multicultural Teams," in Soon Ang and Linn Van Dyne, eds., *Handbook of Cultural Intelligence: Theory, Measurement, and Applications* (Armonk, NY: M.E. Sharpe, 2008), 180.

16. Cheryl Tay, Mina Westman, and Audrey Chia, "Antecedents and Consequences of Cultural Intelligence Among Short-Term Business Travelers," in Soon Ang and Linn Van Dyne, eds., *Handbook of Cultural Intelligence: Theory, Measurement, and Applications* (Armonk, NY: M.E. Sharpe, 2008), 126–144; S. Ang, L. Van Dyne, C. Koh, K. Y. Ng, K. J. Templer, C. Tay, and N. A. Chandrasekar, "Cultural Intelligence: Its Measurement and Effects on Cultural Judgment and Decision Making, Cultural Adaptation, and Task Performance," *Management and Organization Review* 3 (2007): 335–371; L. M. Shannon and T. M. Begley, "Antecedents of the Four-Factor Model of Cultural Intelligence," Soon Ang and Linn Van Dyne, eds., *Handbook of Cultural Intelligence: Theory, Measurement, and Applications* (Armonk, NY: M.E. Sharpe, 2008), 41–55.

17. You Jin Kim and Linn Van Dyne, "A Moderated Mediation Model of Intercultural Contact and Work Overseas Potential: Implications for Selection and Development of Global Leaders" (paper presented at the

annual international meeting for the Society for Industrial Organization Psychology, Atlanta, Georgia, April 8–10, 2010); Kevin Groves, "Leader Cultural Intelligence in Context: Testing the Moderating Effects of Team Cultural Diversity on Leader and Team Performance" (paper presented at the annual international meeting for the Society for Industrial Organization Psychology, Atlanta, Georgia, April 8–10, 2010).

Chapter 4: CQ Knowledge

1. Lee Yih-teen, Aline D. Masuda, and Pablo Cardona, "The Interplay of Self, Host, and Global Cultural Identities in Predicting Cultural Intelligence and Leadership Perception in Multicultural Teams" (paper presented at the annual international meeting for the Society for Industrial Organization Psychology, Atlanta, Georgia, April 8–10, 2010).

2. Linn Van Dyne and Soon Ang, "The Sub-Dimensions of the Four-Factor Model of Cultural Intelligence," Technical Report. Cultural Intelligence Center, 2008.

3. Terrence Linhart, "They Were So Alive: The Spectacle Self and Youth Group Short-Term Mission Trips" (paper presented at the North Central Evangelical Missiological Society Meeting, Deerfield, IL, April 9, 2005), 7.

4. Edna Reid Ph.D., *Intelligence Gathering for Cultural Intelligence* (Singapore: Nanyang Technological University, April 2009).

5. P. C. Earley, C. Murnieks, and Elaine Mosakowski, "Cultural Intelligence and the Global Mindset," *Advances in International Management*, Volume 19 (New York: JAI Press, 2007), 75–103.

6. Daisann McLane, "Moved by the Movies," *National Geographic Traveler* (July–August 2010), 12.

7. In particular, see Chapter 5 of David Livermore, *Leading with Cultural Intelligence* (New York: AMACOM, 2010) for more.

8. Several of these values stem from Geert Hofstede's work. Visit http://www.geert hofstede.com/ to get the ratings for various cultures. For one of the most complete overviews on cultural value dimensions, see R. J. House. P. J. Hanges, M. Javidan, P. W. Dorfman, and V. Gupta, *Culture, Leadership, and Organizations: The GLOBE Study of 62 Societies* (Thousand Oaks, CA: SAGE, 2004).

9. Edward Hall, *Beyond Culture* (New York: Anchor Books, 1981), 39.

10. P. Kay and W. Kempton, "What Is the Sapir-Whorf Hypothesis?" *American Anthropologist* 86, no. 1 (1984): 65–79. And John Carroll, *Language, Thought, and Reality: Selected Writings of Benjamin Lee Whorf* (Cambridge, MA: MIT Press, 1964), 212–214.

11. President Barack Obama, University of Michigan graduation speech, Ann Arbor, MI: University of Michigan, May 1, 2010.
12. Craig Storti, *The Art of Crossing Cultures* (Yarmouth, ME: Intercultural Press, 1990), 72.
13. Joyce Osland and Allan Bird, "Beyond Sophisticated Stereotyping: Cultural Sensemaking in Context," *Academy of Management Executive* 14, no. 1 (2000), 73.

Chapter 5: CQ Strategy

1. Linn Van Dyne and Soon Ang, "The Sub-Dimensions of the Four-Factor Model of Cultural Intelligence," Technical Report, Cultural Intelligence Center, 2008.
2. R. Desimone and J. Duncan, "Neural Mechanisms of Selective, Visual Attention," *Annual Review of Neuroscience* 18 (1995): 193–222.
3. Grant McCracken, *Chief Culture Officer: How to Create a Living, Breathing Corporation* (New York: Basic Books, 2009), 119–120.
4. Gregory David Roberts, *Shantaram* (New York: St. Martins Griffin, 2003), 105.
5. T. F. Pettigrew, "The Ultimate Attribution Error: Extending Allport's Cognitive Analysis of Prejudice," *Personality and Social Psychology Bulletin* 5, no. 4 (1979): 461–476.
6. Jason Fried and David Heinemeier Hansson, *ReWork: Change the Way You Work Forever* (London: Vermilion, 2010), 74.
7. David Rock, *Your Brain at Work: Strategies for Overcoming Distraction, Regaining Focus, and Working Smarter All Day Long* (New York: Harper Collins, 2009), 212.
8. Adapted from mindfulness measures developed by Kirk Warren Brown and Richard M. Ryan, *Mindful Attention Awareness Scale* (MAAS) http://www.psych.rochester.edu/SDT/measures/maas_description.php.
9. Rock, 94.
10. Ibid., 89.
11. William Weeks, Paul Pedersen, and Richard Brislin, *A Manual for Structured Experiences for Cross-Cultural Learning* (Yarmouth, ME: Intercultural Press, 1977), xv.
12. M. F. Mason, M. I. Norton, J. D. Van Horn, D. M. Wegner, S. T. Grafton, and C. N. Macrae. "Wandering Minds: The Default Network and Stimulus-Independent Thought," *Science* 315 (2007): 393–395.
13. Van Dyne and Ang.
14. Rock, 147.

15. Robert Merton, *Social Theory and Social Structure* (New York: Free Press, 1968), 319.

16. K. Templer, C. Tay, and N. A. Chandrasekar, "Motivational Cultural Intelligence, Realistic Job Preview, Realistic Living Conditions Preview, and Cross-Cultural Adjustment," *Group & Organization Management* 31, no. 1 (February 2006): 168.

17. Atul Gawande, *The Checklist Manifesto: How to Get Things Right* (New York: Metropolitan Books, 2009).

18. K. N. Ochsner, R. D. Ray, J. C. Cooper, E. R. Robertson, S. Chopra, and J. D. D. Gabrieli, "For Better or For Worse: Neural Systems Supporting the Cognitive Down and Up-Regulation of Negative Emotion," *Neuroimage* 23, no. 2 (2004): 483–499.

19. M. D. Lieberman, N. I. Eisenberger, M. J. Crockett, S. M. Tom, J. H. Pfiefer, and B. M. Way, "Putting Feelings into Words: Affect Labeling Disrupts Amygdala Activity in Response to Affective Stimuli," *Psychological Science* 18, no. 5 (2007): 421–428.

20. Van Dyne and Ang.

21. Six Sigma Financial Services, "Determine the Root Cause: 5 Whys," http://finance.isixsigma.com/library/content/c020610a.asp (accessed 16 August 2007).

Chapter 6: CQ Action

1. Linn Van Dyne and Soon Ang, "The Sub-Dimensions of the Four-Factor Model of Cultural Intelligence," Technical Report, Cultural Intelligence Center, 2008.

2. Erving Goffman, *The Presentation of Self in Everyday Life* (New York: Anchor Books, 1959).

3. See Terri Morrison, Wayne A. Conaway, and George A. Borden, Ph.D., *Bow, Kiss, or Shake Hands* (Mishawaka, IN: Bob Adams Inc., 1994).

4. Cynthia Beath, Ph.D., Professor Emerita, University of Texas, introduced me to the seventeen famous phrases concept; personal communication, May 2, 2009.

5. Originally reported in my book *Cultural Intelligence: Improving Your CQ to Engage Our Multicultural World* (Grand Rapids: Baker Books, 2008), 115.

6. Efrat Shokef and Miriam Erez, "Cultural Intelligence and Global Identity in Multicultural Teams," in Soon Ang and Linn Van Dyne, eds., *Handbook of Cultural Intelligence: Theory, Measurement, and Applications* (Armonk, NY: M.E. Sharpe, 2008), 177–191.

Chapter 7: The Power of CQ

1. Kok-Yee Ng, Linn Van Dyne, and Soon Ang, "From Experience to Experiential Learning: Cultural Intelligence as a Learning Capability for Global Leader Development," *Academy of Management Learning & Education* 8, no. 4 (2009): 511–526.

2. Elizabeth Liebert, *Changing Life Patterns: Adult Development in Spiritual Direction* (St. Louis, MO: Chalice Press, 2000), 121–122.

3. Donald Schon, *Educating the Reflective Practitioner* (San Francisco: Jossey-Bass, 1987).

4. Ben Bryant and Karsten Jonsen, "Cross-Cultural Leadership: How to Run Operations in Markets We Don't Understand," Switzerland: IMD Business School, October 2008.

5. Karen D. Davis, ed., *Cultural Intelligence and Leadership: An Introduction for Canadian Forces Leaders* (Kingston, Ontario: Canadian Defence Academy Press, 2009), x.

6. "Frontline Females: Unlocking The World of Afghan Women," *International Security Assistance Force Public Affairs Office, Afghanistan* (January 21, 2010), http://www.isaf.nato.int/article/isaf-releases/frontline-females-unlocking-the-world-of-afghan-women.html (accessed July 2, 2010).

7. Davis, x.

8. Which MBA? *The Economist Online* (October 14, 2009), http://www.economist.com/business-education/whichmba/displaystory.cfm?story_id=14536868 (accessed July 2, 2010).

ACKNOWLEDGMENTS

First, thanks to the students and clients around the globe whose feedback and questions gave birth to this book. Just about the time I think I've exhausted what there is to say about cultural intelligence, your questions and ideas push me to see that there's so much more ground to cover.

And thanks to the many individuals who read early drafts of this manuscript. Your encouragement, suggestions, and, most of all, critiques made this a much more worthwhile piece. Thanks especially to Soon Ang, Steve Argue, Brad Griffin, Scott Matthies, Colleen Mizuki, Kara Powell, Elena Steiner, and Linn Van Dyne.

Soon Ang and Linn Van Dyne, it's a joy to call you friends as well as professional partners and colleagues. I ride on the coattails of your ruthless commitment to rigorous research. And thanks to the many other academic colleagues around the world who are advancing the study and application of cultural intelligence into new frontiers.

Christina Parisi, thanks for another round of publishing together. You and the rest of the team at AMACOM are such a joy to work with. And the fact that you personally embrace these ideals is deeply rewarding to me.

Andrew and Lynn, Tandy, Steve, Jen, Rob, and Kristen— thanks for nurturing my soul and believing in me regardless of how this book ever does.

Linda, Emily, and Grace: Your love alone would be enough. But the fact that you so fully join me in the cause of making the world a better place is icing on top. I love you.

RESOURCES
FROM THE CULTURAL INTELLIGENCE CENTER, LLC

The Cultural Intelligence Center (CQC) is dedicated to assessing and developing cultural intelligence worldwide.

- **CQ Assessments:** CQC offers a variety of customized assessments for assessing and developing CQ. Current offerings include the *CQ Multi-Rater Assessment* (360°) and CQ assessments specifically developed for workplace settings, study abroad trips, short-term mission groups, faith-based work, and age-specific groups. CQC also offers the *Individual Cultural Values Inventory*.

- **CQ Certification Programs:** Get certified to use the *CQ Multi-Rater Assessment* (360°) in your organization or as a consultant with other clients.

- **CQ Research:** CQC conducts ongoing research on CQ and is interested in collaborating with other researchers in the field.

- **CQ Consulting and Training:** CQC offers public workshops on CQ and works with organizations to provide customized consulting and training sessions for their employees and constituents.

* * *

Visit www.CulturalQ.com for more information about these offerings.

INDEX

ABOUT THE AUTHOR

David Livermore, Ph.D., is a thought leader in cultural intelligence and global leadership. He's president and partner at the Cultural Intelligence Center in East Lansing, Michigan, and a visiting professor at Nanyang Technological University in Singapore. He's worked with leaders in business, government, and charitable organizations in a hundred countries. He's written several books on global issues and cross-cultural engagement, including *Leading with Cultural Intelligence*. He and his wife, Linda, live with their two daughters in Grand Rapids, Michigan.